More praise for
Elizabeth Harper's
Wishing

"With a unique voice and a down-to-earth approach, Elizabeth Harper's book is a magically spell-binding and timeless addition to anyone's bookshelf."

Jill Dahne,
#1 love psychic in *100 Top Psychics in America*

"Like a breath of fresh air—this book will inspire your deepest desires to become reality—a visionary book that will help define your higher purpose."

Tim Wheater,
award-winning composer and flautist

"*Wishing* is a practical, thorough, and extraordinary guide. Through this book Elizabeth Harper offers a step by step program for unleashing the inner genie in us all: one that is capable of granting our every wish."

Brett Bevell,
author of *The Reiki Magic Guide to Self Attunement*

Wishing

May zero

To Janis

Thank you for sharing
your light~

Best wishes
Elizabeth Hope

Wishing

How to Fulfill Your Heart's Desires

Elizabeth Harper

ATRIA BOOKS
New York London Toronto Sydney

ATRIA BOOKS
A Division of Simon & Schuster, Inc.
1230 Avenue of the Americas
New York, NY 10020

Cynthia Black
Heather Jones →
BEYOND WORDS
PUBLISHING
20827 N.W. Cornell Road, Suite 500
Hillsboro, Oregon 97124-9808
503-531-8700 / 503-531-8773 fax
www.beyondword.com

503-867-9150

Managing editor: Lindsay S. Brown
Editor: Julie Clayton Knowles
Copyeditor: Ali McCart
Proofreader: Meadowlark Publishing Services
Cover and interior design: Sara E. Blum
Composition: William H. Brunson Typography Services

First Atria Books/Beyond Words trade paperback edition May 2008

ATRIA BOOKS and colophon are trademarks of Simon & Schuster, Inc.
Beyond Words Publishing is a division of Simon & Schuster, Inc.

For more information about special discounts for bulk purchases, please contact Simon & Schuster Special Sales at 1-800-456-6798 or business@simonandschuster.com.

Manufactured in the United States of America

10   9   8   7   6   5   4   3   2   1

Library of Congress Cataloging-in-Publication Data:

Harper, Elizabeth.
    Wishing : how to fulfill your heart's desires / Elizabeth Harper. — 1st Atria Books/ Beyond Words trade pbk. ed.
        p.   cm.
    Includes bibliographical references.
    1. Wishes.   2. Magic.   I. Title.

    BF1621.H38   2008
    131—dc22

                                                        2007048163

ISBN-13: 978-1-58270-197-4
ISBN-10:   1-58270-197-0

The corporate mission of Beyond Words Publishing, Inc.: *Inspire to Integrity*

I offer *Wishing* in dedication to all those who
strive to reveal the light, the truth, and the way,
so that no soul is left behind.

Contents

Part IV: Wish Fulfillment

Acknowledgments

My deepest gratitude goes to my husband, Win. I wished for him, and he appeared right on cue. He supports me in all of my work with an unending wisdom and love that exudes from his very being. I am truly blessed to have him in my life.

To my brother Andrew Gosling, who has always been one of the most inspiring forces for me. His encouragement has spurred me on to reach my goals.

To my mother in spirit for her nurturing, wise counsel in my younger years, to my father in spirit for his music and practical support when I most needed it, and to my brother Philip in spirit who guided and protected me in his artist's way.

To my friend and soul sister Denise Giblin, who, during all the years I can remember, has been the most supportive and loving friend that anyone could ever hope to meet.

To all my friends who have painstakingly read my work, given feedback, and heartily given their counsel and support, I thank you— Meg Vecchi, Rich Warren, Virginia Pasternak, Christine VanCoughnet, Melissa Morris, Chrystal Kubis, Lois Guarino, and Finton Coyle.

To my dear friend Kari Samuels, who guides me in many areas of my life and work, watching over me like a long-lost mother. I am so grateful for her guidance and support. She led me to my wonderful agent, Regina Brooks, who gracefully dances through her work, knowingly touching exactly the right people with just a welcome amount of sparkle.

To my exceptional editor, Julie Clayton, who has the ability to see all sides of the same story and blend it into something fabulous and extraordinary. Without her editing skills, this book would not be what it is today. My book was ready to be born, and Julie is the gifted literary midwife.

To my remarkable editor-in-chief Cynthia Black, who touched me the moment I spoke with her. Her vision and gift is discovering uniquely spiritual topics that make people sit up and take notice. I am so honored that she singled out my book to be a part of her family.

To the team at Beyond Words—Publisher Richard Cohn, Lindsay Brown, Marie Hix, Rachel Berry, Lisa Dubbels, and Courtney Dunham—who together present a united force in the publishing world, yet remain so personable. I am blessed to have their support and encouragement.

To my friends and colleagues at Omega, Aviana, Stonewater Sanctuary, and Opal Moon who supported my work early in my career in the United States. Their belief in my skills as a teacher and the opportunities they have presented have helped me to achieve my deepest wishes and my purpose.

To Matthew Manning, a good friend and an incredible healer who steered me on a course inward to discover myself. He could see potential gifts in me that I was unaware of, and I am grateful to him for lighting the way.

Finally, to all those who are attracted to this book, I thank you for giving me the chance to share my insight and understanding of wishing with you. Know that there are no coincidences. Your heart sang out, and this book is a reflection of that tune. It contains the energy that will guide you to manifest your truest and deepest wishes.

How to Use This Book...

Make a wish. Now close your eyes and imagine that whatever you have wished for is in your life right now. How does it feel?

You have the opportunity to make all of your wishes come true. Wishing is the act of invoking energy to manifest your heart's desire. There are seven simple steps in the process of successful wishing, which I call *wish sense*. Wish sense is an ancient art of turning wishes into reality, but one that does not rely on superstition or old wives' tales. Rather, wish sense is based on tried and tested principles for achieving a desired outcome.

Now, take a piece of paper or a card and write at the top, "My wish is ..." Take a moment to compose your thoughts. If you had just one wish to make, something you would like in your life that would enhance or improve it, what would it be? When you have decided on a wish, write it on the paper, then seal it in an envelope and place it somewhere special, such as next to your bed, on a mirror, or on an altar. Sealing your wish in the envelope will discourage you from changing it as you work through the book. At times you will be prompted to review your wish, but it is beneficial to wait until you have completed the book before changing or altering your wish in any way.

There are seven easy steps to making a wish come true. They are revealed in this book through the rediscovery of your individual creative power. It is important to work through the book sequentially and not be tempted to skip to the end. Practice the exercises given in each chapter before moving on. Keep a wish journal of your insights, recording your thoughts and experiences as you expand your awareness. Use separate pages for each exercise, numbering them for easy reference. Once you have written down your thoughts, you will begin to edit them for relevant facts, which I will guide you through. This will help you to identify repeated or similar themes and assist you in organizing your wishes and desires.

Wishing is designed to help you to recognize your own ability to manifest your wishes, as well as demonstrate why some wishes fall on rocky soil. By following the principles of wish sense, you will learn how to manifest your wishes and, most importantly, how to get exactly what you need to live a happy and wish-fulfilled life. After all, you deserve everything the universe has to offer. Now is the time to take control of your life, to realize your dreams, to actualize your heart's desires, and to manifest your wishes. I offer you the best of wishes on this journey...

Introduction

*To wish is to feel an impulse toward attainment
or possession of something.*
—*Random House College Dictionary*

I wrote *Wishing* after an occurrence involving my husband, Win. He was about to go on a solo camping trip but realized that one essential item was missing: an outdoor grill. Reminiscing about previous camping trips with friends reminded him of the things he most liked about spending time outdoors. He remembered the wonderful walks, the beautiful colors of the trees, the fragrant smell of nature, and the people he met along the way. He recalled the delicious meals that were freshly cooked on a grill. It was this particular memory that was most tantalizing, and Win decided to immediately purchase his own barbecue equipment for his upcoming trip.

The very next day there was a knock on the front door. It was a neighbor who had been clearing out her attic and had come across an item she thought Win could put to good use. It was an outdoor barbecue, exactly what he needed and wanted for his trip. He was so taken aback by this manifestation of his desire that he accused me of having something to do with it, protesting, "You are the only person this kind of thing happens to!"

You probably know as well as I do that the above situation is far from unique since "this kind of thing" happens to most people on occasion. However, over the years I have become more aware of how to make wishes come true and why some do not manifest. I wanted to share this knowledge with others by writing a book about wish sense.

However, this was a task that initially proved to be easier said than done. Expressing my spiraling thoughts with pen and paper was time-consuming, and I quickly realized that writing a book would be challenging, if not impossible, without a computer. The glitch was that I did not own one, nor at that time could I afford to buy one. Still, I was undeterred by my dilemma, especially in view of my past experiences with wish sense.

The day after I made the decision to begin writing, I literally found a free computer, in full working order. It was at my workplace in an area where people would deposit unwanted or unsalable items. It had been left by a generous stranger who undoubtedly had recently bought a new, updated computer and, having no further use for his old model, thought it might serve a purpose elsewhere. In my wildest dreams I could not have imagined receiving a computer in this way. As part of the wish sense process, I had let go of my need to control events and was able to receive with open arms the abundance available to me. (I explain more about letting go and abundance later in the book.)

I was truly delighted to receive my wish so quickly! But there is no telling how long a wish will take to manifest. Sometimes wishes can take minutes, hours, days, or even years.

The techniques in this book are based on my experience, common sense, ancient practices, Eastern philosophies, and the now-familiar law of attraction. I will explain in detail how to make all of your wishes come true. Allow yourself to be receptive to the information contained within the book. The wisdom of wish sense will assist you in manifesting everything you have ever wished for. Open your heart and mind to the abundance of the universe, and join me on this magical journey of self-discovery.

Part I

Crafting Your Wish

Everything is optional, anything is possible,
just ask for what you want.

—Sandwich board in Red Hook, New York

1

A Wish in Time

If wishes were horses, beggars would ride.
—English proverb (from a collection of proverbs
published by John Ray in 1670)

When was the last time you made a wish? Was it on your birthday when you blew out the candles on your cake, or when you saw a shooting star traveling through the sky, or the last time you had turkey for dinner and split the wishbone with someone? Can you recall making a wish on a coin and afterward tossing it into a fountain or a stream? Before your initiation into wish sense, let us first explore some of these ancient wishing techniques.

Numerous systems for divining wishes are available. Many are steeped in archaic wisdom or are the result of local traditions, yet others reveal the core essence of wish sense. Over time, both others and I have adapted some of these traditional methods for modern-day usage.

For example, one of the most important ingredients in wish sense is letting a wish go. When you make a wish on your birthday, or on a shooting star, or on a dandelion head, the common factors involved begin with focusing on the wish and then letting it go. Blowing out candles directs your focus toward blowing the wish into the fire and then releasing it when the fire is extinguished. Wishing on a shooting star is similar in that you transfer your wish onto something that is present for only a brief moment in time. Once the star's light is extinguished or out of sight, then the wish sense ritual is finished. A wish on a dandelion concludes when the seeds are blown into the wind. In each case there is an end point to the wish. You make the wish and then let it go.

The art of wish sense embraces the positive components of folklore rituals. Over time, it is the less-than-positive aspect of folklore—superstition—that has mostly been remembered. Superstition is essentially founded upon fear. We have embraced age-old superstitions in many aspects of our lives, deeming them lucky or unlucky omens. Walking under a ladder is thought to be unlucky. A black cat crossing your path augurs luck, provided it is walking in a particular direction: toward you is good luck, away from you it takes the luck with it, from right to left brings bad fortune, and from left to right good fortune. For a bride, it is considered unlucky for the groom to see her wearing her wedding dress before the big day. On the day of her wedding, she will invite luck to bless her upcoming nuptials by seeking out something old, something new, something borrowed, and something blue. Old wives' tales and superstitions are defined as fear-based beliefs that have been established by practice, opinion, or religion.

In contrast, wish sense is not based in fear; it is built upon the natural laws of attraction, manifestation, and cause and effect. Wish sense is unconnected to luck. Instead, it is shaped by your own individual creative power. You will learn more about your creative power in chapter 2.

Birthday Wishes

Most of us have performed the centuries-old candle magic custom of blowing out the candles on a birthday cake while making a wish. Although this well-established ritual is probably derived from an ancient Greek custom, no one is certain where it first originated. The modern wish sense process associated with this classic practice is based on the power of three ingredients: the focus (concentrating on the lighted candles), the wish (visualized onto the candles), and the magic (blowing your wish away with the flame). As with most wish-related superstitions, the birthday wish will be granted provided it is kept secret and not divulged to anyone else.

Birthday Spell

Most people are familiar with the birthday candle ritual, but not all are aware that the precise time of your birth is the most powerful moment to make a birthday wish. If you know the time of day you were born, then make a special wish at this time on your birthday for the coming year. Write your wish on a card and place it in an envelope to remain unopened for one year. Put the envelope in a place where it will receive energy, such as on a mirror or attached to wind chimes. This way the energy of your wish will be increased. At the end of the year, perform a burning ritual: read the card again, and then burn the contents to release your wish into the universe.

You can make this event even more special by performing a sacred ceremony. First, create an altar to your wish using fresh flowers, candles, and incense. Place some pictures or images of your manifested wish on the altar. Use music to generate the right atmosphere. Include anything that you feel will invoke a sense of specialness. Once you have created your altar, position a candle in the center, and when you are ready to begin your card-burning ceremony, light the candle, ask it to take your wish into the ethers, read your wish aloud, and then offer the paper it is written on to the flame. Ensure that you perform this ritual in a well-aired room and away from flammable objects. Let your paper burn right through, and then take the ashes outside and scatter them to the wind. When you extinguish the candle, say thank you.

Candle Magic

Wishes and spells are fueled by candle magic, characterized by the burning of candles to shape the future. Candles have been used since Paleolithic times. The flame represents the spark of life or the fire of creation. The ritual use of candles may have been a form of ancient fire worship, honoring the light of the soul as an aspect of the greater fire of creativity—the Divine, or God. When a candle is freshly lit, it symbolically represents birth and new beginnings. If a candle is used in any kind of wish sense ritual, it furthers its creation and ultimate manifestation by invoking the aid of the light of God.

In Celtic Britain, during the pagan festival of Beltane on May Eve, women who wished to become pregnant would jump over the Beltane fires, assuring them greater success in their pursuit of a productive outcome. Due to their shape, candles were considered to be phallic symbols. Hence, a woman wishing to get pregnant could expect a more favorable outcome by jumping over a lighted candle, its symbolism further supporting the objective.

Candle Spells

Burning candles is a wonderful way to perform a wish ritual, and the different colors of candles symbolize specific gifts. My studies in the various branches of color therapy training gave me great insight into color's traditional significance. A green candle, for instance, is burned to encourage increased abundance and health. Pink candles invoke love and romance, whereas blue encourages inspiration, communication, and healing. Violet is the color of transformation and spirituality; violet candles can be used to clear unwanted energy and encourage positive change. Purple represents passion, red is for security and work, orange signifies creativity and children, and yellow denotes joy and the intellect. White, symbolizing purity and peace, can be used in any situation and imbued with the desire of the invoker.

When making a wish, hold the candle and infuse it with positive vibrations. Picture in your mind what you want to achieve. While the candle burns, imagine the flame is the light of the universe taking your wish into the heavens. Allow it to burn down to the end, and dispose of the remaining wick with love. Give thanks not only to the universe but also to the energy of the candle for aiding in your quest.

When You Wish Upon a Star

Many superstitions are derived from the ancient Celtic lore of paganism, the religion of the old way (pagan comes from the Latin word *paganus*, meaning country dweller). In pagan mythology the stars and planets were thought to be human souls. As a child I was led to believe that the sun was the physical body of a great spirit: a myth that probably dates back to the worship of the luminaries. Spells, the secret magic of ancient lore, have been passed down through the ages in the form of poems and nursery rhymes. One still-popular childhood rhyme reveals a spell for making wishes on the first star detected in the evening sky:

Star light, star bright,
The first star I see tonight,
I wish I may, I wish I might,
Have the wish I wish tonight.

Observing the star while reciting the poem will increase the potency of the wish and guarantee its success. Like most spells, the poem contains a catchy rhyme similar to an affirmation, which is part of its enchantment. A shooting star was thought to represent birth, a soul passing from heaven to earth. As a symbol of birth, it was open to be wished upon, but the wisher had to be quick, as the charm would only work while the star remained visible in the sky.

Moonstruck Wishes

The moon plays a large part in many superstitions. When it comes to the ancient practice of wish sense, there are laws involving the lunar cycle. The period from new to full moon is called the waxing moon. This is the optimal time to make your wishes and to cast spells for something to grow. The waning moon, the period from full to new, is perfect for removing or decreasing the energy of something in your life. Have your hair cut on the waxing moon to make it grow faster, and mow the lawn on a waning moon to stunt its growth. The period from the end of the moon cycle to the next new moon is known as the dark moon. This was the time when witches and wizards would cast spells to manipulate the thoughts and actions of others. Be aware that the negative use of universal energy is recorded in time. This means that one day you will have to account for your actions.

Moonstruck Nature Spell

Do you remember making a wish on a dandelion, blowing on the downy seed head, thus propelling the seeds into the air along with your wish? Planting seeds infused with your wish is a wonderful way to nurture its manifestation. Tapping into the natural flow of the universe increases your wish power. An excellent way to utilize this is by placing the energy of your wish into a flower bulb or seeds, and then planting them at the time of the new moon. As the plant grows and blossoms, so will your wish.

Well Wishing

Most people, at some time in their lives, will have thrown a coin into a well and made a wish. Springs and wells were home to water goddesses, sprites, and fairies. The wishing well probably owes its origins to the belief that the residents of the well had magical powers and were capable of making wishes come true. The traditional offering

of a coin in exchange for a wish was a form of prayer to the guardian of the waters. In ancient times, anything made from metal—such as swords, bowls, or goblets—would be offered to urge the guardians to share their powers. When some wells made strange noises, it was thought to be a warning of impending disaster. Other watery places, such as the waters of Lourdes in France and the Chalice Well of Glastonbury in England, are supposed to possess healing properties. One famous well at St. Elian in Llanelian-yn-Rhos, Wales, has a reputation for making curses come true. The supernatural power of the well-keeper is invoked by a written request placed in a lead casket and lowered into the well. Beware of making curses, however, as it is well known in ancient wish sense practices that a curse will be returned thrice-fold to the curser.

Fairy Wishes

Fairies are featured in many old stories, now called fairy tales; two of the most famous fairies are Cinderella's fairy godmother and Peter Pan's fairy, Tinker Bell. All fairies are capable of meting out wishes. Probably the most sought-after wish comes from the tooth fairy, who overnight replaces your tooth with a token of good faith, usually a coin. Once the token is returned to the fairy, your wish will be granted.

But how do you find a fairy? According to magical lore, a fairy ring signified the sacred meeting place of both fairies and witches. Fairy rings can be found in two different forms: in a ring of dark grass caused by fungi or in a mixture of mushrooms, predominantly red with white spots—a variety most often associated in England with garden gnomes. If the center of the ring is stepped into by mistake, the trespasser could be in jeopardy of losing his or her soul to the world of the fairies. On the other hand, legend declares that if someone stands in a fairy ring under a full moon and makes a wish, the wish will be granted.

Three Wishes

In Ireland, a tree in the center of a field is considered inhabited by fairies, and it is bad luck to cut it down. The Irish also have a firm belief in the little people. Where else could the leprechaun be a national symbol? The classic movie *Finian's Rainbow* is a tale about a man who happens upon a leprechaun while searching for a pot of gold at the end of a rainbow. When a leprechaun is caught, the price he has to pay for his freedom is to grant three wishes. The leprechaun tries to trick Finian into making his wishes quickly, but Finian holds the leprechaun captive while he considers his options. He is slow to make his wishes since he appreciates how essential it is to make a wish in the correct way.

There are many instances where the number three is included in the magic formula for wish sense. Three is known to be a powerful number in numerology, representing the planet Jupiter—symbolizing abundance, expansion, and luck—and the trinity, or the three stages of a human: father/mother/child; father/son/holy ghost; virgin/mother/crone. Whenever a fourth wish was made, the previous three would be dis-spelled.

The Thrice-fold Spell

For this spell, write down what you want in simple terms and then state your wish verbally three times. As you say your wish, visualize it becoming a reality. Use a candle to help you to invoke a sense of specialness. Each time you speak the wish out loud, draw your arms around the lighted candle and bring the energy of your wish toward your heart. Capture the essence of your wish in your heart and imagine that you already have what you want in your life. When you have finished, take a moment to breathe in the energy of your wish and then say thank you for its ultimate manifestation.

Wishing in Pairs

In bygone days, the well-known tradition of pulling the wishbone was to discover who would marry first. The wishbone, or merry-thought, is a forked or V-shaped bone obtained from between the neck and breast of a bird. Customarily, two people are chosen to pull the wishbone. While pulling either end, a secret wish is made, but only the winner of the longer portion will have his or her wish fulfilled. Another wish involving a couple occurs when two people say the same thing at the same time. They are supposed to lock fingers together before uttering another word, right hand to right hand or left to left, and make a silent wish. The wish will only come true if nothing is said until the fingers are released.

Spitting Out Your Wish

In many parts of the world it is still customary to spit when making a wish. Spittle was thought to be the heart of soul power and therefore a potent instrument of magic and protection. In Greece spitting three times is still used to remove the curse of the evil eye. The horseshoe, thought to symbolically represent the shape of the new crescent moon and known for centuries as an amulet of luck, is made wish-worthy by first spitting on it. Once the wish is made, the shoe should then be thrown over the left shoulder (after making sure no one is standing behind) and without looking back, the wisher walks away. If a piece of coal, symbolizing abundance, is given as a gift, it should be spat on before being thrown into a burning fire. Subsequently, a wish is made while the coal burns.

A Pinch of Salt

Salt was a valuable commodity during ancient times, both as a preservative for meats and a cleansing agent. It is still often used as a protective agent in ritual magic. If laid in a circle around an individual, it can guard against malevolent spirits or negativity. When salt is spilled, a few grains should be taken in the right hand and, once a wish has been made, immediately thrown over the left shoulder.

The cleansing effect of salt can also be useful to rid one-self of daily grime. When you cleanse yourself with salt, you will feel both physically and spiritually lighter. The old saying "cleanliness is next to godliness" may have derived from this very concept. Put Epsom salts into your bath or rub salt on your body while taking a shower. Imagine that the saltwater is cleansing you both on the inside and the outside.

Super Wish Sense

Each wish technique in this chapter has an ingredient of wish sense within it. I commented earlier on the focus-and-letting-go elements of candle magic, birthday wishes, and wishing upon a star, but what of the other systems? Many of these methods employ the rhythms of nature, such as moon cycles, or nature itself, such as water in a wishing well. Some involve repeating the wish three times or depend upon a person winning the right to make a wish. In each case, the wish is released with the silent knowledge that it can manifest at any time. You can certainly experiment by bringing aspects of these traditional rituals into your own wish sense practice.

All of the wish sense techniques described in this chapter can be used to attract things you desire. However, sometimes these techniques will not work for a number of reasons: the energy behind the wish was not focused in the right way, the wish was imprecise, the wrong method was applied, you were preventing the wish from materializing, it's not the right time, and so forth. Before your introduction to the seven principles of wish sense, you need to be aware of why you are making the wish and the things that will prevent your wish from materializing.

A few years ago, I had the chance to start a master's degree program, but the costly education fees and the money I would have to earn just to survive made the opportunity unrealistic. Nonetheless, I was unwilling to give up on something I thought would enhance my career. I knew how to make my wishes manifest, and yet I was unable to manifest the abundance I required; I could not understand why.

Two of my friends had consulted a feng shui expert—someone who surveys a space and makes recommendations to rearrange or enhance an area in order to create an optimum energetic environment. Once the changes suggested had been instigated, one of my friends was unexpectedly offered a promotion, while the other, an actor, suddenly had more job offers than he could handle. They told me that apart from some reorganization of the furniture, the expert had recommended crystals to be placed at strategic points in their respective homes. I arranged a consultation for myself, anticipating that a few extra crystals in my abundance corner would probably do the trick.

The feng shui expert inspected my home and made recommendations to totally rearrange my living space and to position crystals in specific corners of each room. Without a second thought, I threw myself into transforming my home into an abundance altar. A month passed and nothing happened. I called him to ask why there had been no change; he told me to wait another month. I waited and still nothing happened, so he decided to inspect my work. After surveying my home for a second time, he concluded that I was resisting the change. I could hardly believe my ears—why on earth would I resist abundance? Why would anyone resist abundance? And yet his words rang true.

Regardless of what I did externally, I would not be able to manifest the abundance I desired until I implemented change within myself. I was trying to achieve something by changing my outer world, whereas I should have been focusing on transforming my inner world. The next day I made an appointment with a psychotherapist. Over time, I worked on my inner world. I became aware that my internal changes were mirrored by drastic changes in my outer life. I did not take the master's degree; I realized that I had been focusing on the wrong thing. Instead, I focused on what I really wanted, which was to work as a therapist. This experience of focusing my heart on what I truly wanted enhanced my understanding of wish sense.

2

The Blueprints
for Your Wishes

It is easier to behave your way into a
new way of thinking than it is to think your way
into a new way of behaving.

—Anonymous

Do you remember your childhood fantasies? Were you the
princess who found her prince and lived happily ever after? Or
were you the superhero who saved the world from evil warriors and
mass destruction? Do you remember the dreams you had for your
future? Did you know what you were going to be when you grew up?
Were you going to change the world and do things differently, be
somebody? Did you know what you did and did not want in your
life? Are you living your dream right now? Do you have everything
you want in your life?

In wish sense it is important to remember your dreams and to keep
track of how many of them have been realized. For instance, my husband loved to play the superhero. He was either Hopalong Cassidy
or Superman. He even wore his Superman outfit underneath his
school uniform. As an adult he chose to enter the military, a career
that embodied his superhero fantasy. This time, however, he really
was in a position to save the world.

Our childhood fantasies are not always that far from the truth of
our dreams for the future. I wanted to heal people, so I became a
nurse. Knowing and taking the steps required to make your wishes
come true will help you to consciously manifest those dreams.

15

Dreams

Psychologist Sigmund Freud claimed that the essence of our nocturnal dreams represented the fulfillment of a conscious or unconscious wish, and he called this "wish fulfillment." In other words, when we dream of what we want, the wish is realized in the dream—fulfilled—while in reality what we want still remains a dream. Fortunately, we've learned a lot about making dreams come true since Freud's time.

And where would we be without our waking dreams? The late, great animator and film producer, Walt Disney, who brought the magical world of fantasy to life for many children and adults alike, said, "Somehow I can't believe that there are any heights that can't be scaled by a man who knows the secrets of making dreams come true."

How often do you dream of doing something or going someplace and then, with apparently no effort on your part, the opportunity presents itself? You might be tempted to classify this as a coincidence. I would like to suggest another perspective—you made a wish! Is that such a surprise to you? You may even have said, "I wish I could go there," or "I wish I could do this or that." We all make wishes. Some are cast on rocky soil, whereas others come to full bloom as if by magic. So, what is the magical formula for a successful wish?

Acknowledging that you have the power to create whatever you want in life is your first step to making your wishes come true. However, most recipes for success involve more than one ingredient, and this is no exception.

Creative Power

I realized from an early age that if I wished hard enough for something, and then forgot about it, it could manifest within weeks, but if I constantly yearned for something, such as a relationship, it would remain an elusive dream. Without being aware of it, you probably do this every day of your life in some form or another. You may think that it is a mere coincidence, a stroke of luck, or a twist of fate. Consider this for a moment: you have the power to create whatever you want in your life, and the manifestation of your wish is an expression of this skill. I invite you to join me in honoring this talent by calling it your creative power.

Creative power is an ability that is within everyone, and yet mastering this art can sometimes take a change of focus. Imagine that you are looking at a three-dimensional picture: a mass of dots on a piece of paper that occasionally appears to form a shape. All it takes to see the image within the picture is a change of focus. Some people can always see the image, and yet surprisingly, there are others who are unable to make the transition from a mass of dots to a three-dimensional picture. The ability is there, but as anyone knows who can see these pictures, it is just a case of focusing on the right spot and in the right way. This is the same with wish sense. Sometimes a wish takes a change of focus.

We make wishes every day, but not all of them are realized. For example: wishing the train would come on time, wishing for a parking spot, wishing a certain item of clothing will still be available in the store in the right size, wishing for a new job, home, relationship, life, and of course, every week as a nation we wish for six little numbers in the lottery to irrevocably change our lives.

Have you ever wondered why you do not get what you wish for? Whenever you make a wish, you think it is the one thing that will make you happy, but if it isn't coming true, maybe you are just wishing for the wrong thing, or perhaps there is a deeper wish that you are unaware of for the moment. In order for wish sense to be a success, your focus needs to be directed toward your true wish, one that comes from your heart.

Designer Wishes

Where do your wishes come from? Take some time to reflect on your original wish. What inspired you to make this wish above all others? The fundamental key to wish sense is designing your "true wish." There are no right, wrong, true, or false wishes, but some wishes serve your highest good better than others and, as a result, are more likely to manifest. Recognizing the initial source of a wish and understanding the motivations behind it will help you to gain insight into why you are making the wish in the first place. This deeper awareness will support you in designing your true wish by revealing what you really want and by avoiding wishes that might be obstructed. Without this understanding you may well continue to make wishes that are unfulfilled.

A close friend of mine, Faith, dearly wished to have a husband and child. She grew up in a large family and naturally expected to continue in the footsteps of her parents, but her relationships had not turned out quite the way she had hoped. After kissing a few frogs, none of which turned into princes, she resigned herself to believing that her wish for a suitable partner was nothing but a fantasy. She was not in a relationship and did not want to adopt as a single parent. Still, she longed to have a child. And she held her faith that there was a good reason for this longing.

So she changed her focus to wishing for a baby, rather than for a relationship with a man, and then asked herself why she wanted a child. She realized that she wanted to be loved and accepted for herself, and she believed that a child would do this for her. In reality, she needed to love and accept herself first. Faith decided to work on this issue through counseling. Not long after her counseling ended, she met someone and was able to open her heart to a loving relationship with him. After only a few months together, they adopted a baby. This little bundle of joy was a mirror that reflected all the energy of love and acceptance she had been seeking and had found already within herself.

Consider this: if you wish for a promotion at work, is it because you seek approval, respect, more money, or greater power? A simple way to determine the motivation behind your wish is by applying a question-and-answer format to your wish. First, though, you have to ask yourself, "What do I want?" Although this sounds simplistic and obvious, it's surprising how rarely we take the time to truly inquire into our heart's desires for our true wish. Throughout this book you will find exercises I call Wish Practice that you can use right away to achieve your wish.

WISH PRACTICE:
The Why Exercise

★ ⋆ ★ ⋆ ☆ ⋆ ☆ ⋆ ☆ ⋆ ★ ⋆ ☆ ⋆ ☆ ⋆ ☆ ⋆ ★ ⋆ ☆ ⋆ ☆ ⋆ ☆

Once you know what to wish for, the following exercise will take your answer a step further. It will help you to discover the emotions and beliefs that are hidden behind the wish.

The question to ask of yourself is, "Why?" With each answer, continue to ask why until you can go no further. The final answer is the source of your motivation.

Continuing with the example of wishing for a promotion, the question-and-answer format might go something like this:

"Why do I want this promotion?"
"Because I want more money."
"Why do I want more money?"
"Because I want to be able to have more material things."
"Why do I want more material things?"
"Because I want to feel more secure."
"Why do I want to feel more secure?"
"Because I want to be secure."

Often a word that is repeated at least twice indicates the deeper motivation. In this case, *security* is the definitive response and therefore the key to the wish. Understanding the initial motivation could change the way the wish is designed, or even change the focus of the wish. If a wish does not manifest, use this question-and-answer technique to determine the motivation behind it and change the wish accordingly. Knowing what you truly want is the key to designing your true wish.

Of course the motivation may not be a neat package simply containing one word. It could be a general feeling, sense, or essence that your wish is based upon. I am someone who tends to connect more with my feelings than with words, at least initially. If you are a feeling person too, then this exercise may result in a stream of words all attempting to convey that feeling. Just know that once you get to that motivation, whether a word or a feeling, then arriving at that point will give you some clarity on the driving force behind your wish.

☆ ⋆ ★ ⋆ ☆ ⋆ ☆ ⋆ ☆ ⋆ ★ ⋆ ☆ ⋆ ☆ ⋆ ☆ ⋆ ★ ⋆ ☆ ⋆ ☆ ⋆ ☆

Now try this Why exercise for yourself and notice how much deeper into the initial wish you can go. Remember to first ask yourself, "What do I want?" and then ask, "Why (do I want this)?" Try this with a simple wish first. Before going into this exercise, it would be beneficial to close your eyes, take a few deep breaths, and relax your mind and body. This will help to center you and calm your emotions, and when you are relaxed it is easier to access authentic answers to your questions. Once you are confident that you can work through this exercise, try it again with the wish you made at the beginning of the book. It is important to be honest with yourself. No one is going to judge you for the reasons behind your wish. We all have unexamined motives, and this is just a tool to discover the driving force behind a wish.

Beliefs and Habits

Now you know the motivation behind your wish. The next step is finding out when and why it originated. This is a useful undertaking, particularly since many of us are motivated by unwanted habits or worn-out concepts that we acquired during our formative years, or even later in life. Addictions, for example, generally take hold later in life. Any habit that is not totally under your voluntary control displays an addictive element. So if your addiction is shopping, your wish might involve buying new things. If addiction is the basis for your wish, then you do not necessarily need something new, and ultimately the creative power required to manifest the wish will not be present.

If your wish is based on a worn-out concept, you might again be asking for something that is already a part of your life. The difference is that the source of your wish comes from a belief that either is no longer relevant or was never true. For instance, if you believe that you do not have enough money and your wishing for more doesn't yield any results, then you are probably harboring a worn-out concept or belief that it is not okay for you to have more money. The worn-out concept of this wish is an underlying belief that money, or abundance, is not currently available to you or is out of your reach, that you do not deserve it or are not worthy of it, or even that life has to be a struggle—and for that reason acquiring wealth also has to be a struggle. We are usually unaware of such worn-out beliefs until we make some effort to uncover them.

One man I used to work with complained that he was constantly in debt, and yet he always seemed to have enough money. Regardless, he tried a variety of techniques to manifest more abundance in his life—prayers, candle magic, and visualization were some of the methods he utilized—but nothing satisfied his need for more money. Then one day he had an insight. Although he had come from a wealthy family, his parents had taught him to be frugal; they believed that money should be saved and not spent on frivolous things such as enjoyment. Consequently, he believed that he needed more money in order to enjoy his life and yet more was never enough.

He began to think about what his life might be like if he let go of his fear of scarcity. He knew that he wanted his freedom from scarcity, and he recognized that he associated money with freedom—a legacy from his parents. With this thought in mind, he realized that he had been asking for the wrong thing. Instead of wishing for money, he should have been wishing for freedom. As soon as he focused his attention on manifesting freedom in his life, he let go of his fear of scarcity, opened his heart to success, and automatically created more abundance in his life. His success has continued to grow, and he currently owns three homes, travels the world for enjoyment, and remains one of the most prosperous people I know.

Beliefs and habits have to begin somewhere. The upcoming exercise can be used to determine the source of your behavior. Discovering where and when your habits and beliefs originated will help you to understand why you are making a wish, which in turn may facilitate your plan for your true wish. The belief or beliefs behind your motivation could have been conceived at any time of your life and for any number of reasons.

Go back to the final answer you received when you asked yourself why you want to make this particular wish. You may already be aware of an earlier incident or experience that created your need for this in your life. If not, then to discover the source of this desire, you can use a technique called writing with your nondominant hand, which I'll explain shortly.

If you can recall the initial incident that created or contributed to your belief without using this exercise, then see if you can also access your feelings from that time. Your feelings are a large factor in the successful manifestation of your wishes and dreams. They are a powerhouse of energy and can effectively advance or oppose your wish. You may have already connected with the emotional impetus behind your wish in the Why exercise. If you did, then you will better understand the motivation behind it.

Writing with Your Nondominant Hand

The exercise of writing with your nondominant hand will help you to uncover where and when your wishes originated. It is well known that the two hemispheres of the brain, left and right, perform different tasks. Experiments have shown that the two sides of the brain interpret information in different ways—the left uses logic and reason, whereas the right applies creative tools such as visual thinking and intuition. The hand you write with normally is called your dominant hand, and the one you use least is your nondominant hand. In this exercise, using your nondominant hand will help you to gain access to internal information while bypassing the analysis of the left brain, irrespective of the left brain's writing function. In fact, just holding the pen in your nondominant hand can stimulate a surprising response.

WISH PRACTICE:
Nondominant Hand Writing

☆ ★ ★ ☆ ★ ☆ ★ ☆ ★ ★ ★ ☆ ★ ☆ ★ ☆ ★ ★ ★ ☆ ★ ☆ ★ ☆

Take a blank piece of paper and, using your dominant hand, write two headings: When did my need for/to be [insert wish or habit] originate? Why did it originate?

For example, let's return to the earlier example and say your wish is for a promotion. Using the Why exercise, you learned that your motivation behind this wish is for security. The question you want to ask yourself now in this next step is: When did my need for security originate?

Before answering the question, take a few moments to relax. Relaxation stimulates the right side of the brain. Close your eyes, take a few deep breaths, and imagine that you are connecting to an all-knowing expression of your creative power. With each breath you take, you become more and more centered in this wise aspect of yourself. When you are ready, write your answers under the headings, this time using your nondominant hand. Do not edit the words or have any preconceived ideas; just allow your thoughts to flow without judgment.

If your ideas don't seem to flow, you can try holding the pen in your nondominant hand and imagine writing the answers— what comes to mind? Alternatively, use your imagination to access the memory banks of your mind. Meditate on the question and visualize the answers. You could imagine writing the answers or visualize someone such as a younger or older version of you sharing the answers with you.

Recognizing the origin of a motivation will help you to understand the ultimate potential for success or failure of your wish. If your wish is based in destructive habits or worn-out concepts, this exercise will assist you in becoming aware of where and when they originated. Using this knowledge will enable you to change behavior that has hindered you for too long. The next section will assist you further on your journey of self-discovery.

☆ ⋆ ★ ⋆ ☆ ⋆ ⋆ ☆ ⋆ ⋆ ☆ ⋆ ★ ⋆ ☆ ⋆ ⋆ ☆ ⋆ ⋆ ★ ⋆ ☆ ⋆ ⋆ ☆ ⋆ ☆

It's Just a Phase!

Have you heard the expression "It's just a phase they're going through"? Our wishes change as experience teaches us the wisdom to identify what is most important in our lives. This transformative process follows the growth experience from childhood, through adolescence, and into adulthood. Your wishes can reflect the objectives of one or more of the following life phases:

Childhood

Objective: As children we are often motivated by immediate needs. Once satisfied, we move on and direct energy toward another goal.

Reflection: A wish made from this period of growth is usually an instant-gratification wish, one that is not intended to stand the test of

 time. This means that your adult wish may be hampered by lingering and subconscious memories of not getting what you wanted as a child. If your wish is not granted immediately, notice the feelings or behavior you may experience when asking for your wish. If you recognize your inner child, then take a deep breath, acknowledge its presence, and let go of the needy feeling. You are powerful beyond measure and no longer need to throw a tantrum to get what you want out of life.

Keywords: Security, Negotiation, Desire, Want, Novelty, Praise

Adolescence

Objective: The confusion of changing hormones, choices to make, and the call of the heart are the primary motivators of the adolescent.

Reflection: A wish made from this stage of life might express itself as a conflict between the heart and mind, love and obsession, right and wrong, and so forth. If you make a wish that you believe will change your life, such as a long-term relationship or a new career path, be aware of the yearnings of your inner adolescent. Particular feelings that may surface are wanting something or someone that is not yours to want or holding on to something that is redundant.

Keywords: Approval, Equilibrium, Belonging, Passion, Craving, Permission

Adulthood

Objective: An adult's motivation is a sophisticated mixture of demands based on current trends, desires of the heart, wealth, and the x-factor—a mysterious element that we know will make us happy and yet appears to be beyond our grasp.

Reflection: As an adult, you are the sum total of your experiences. Therefore, an adult-stage wish will likely reflect issues concerning your experiences of security (child), the latest fashion (adolescent), practicality (adult), love (child), soul mates (adolescent), sex (adult), money (adult), and so on. This does not make the wish any more unattainable; it can just take a little longer to manifest.

Keywords: Stability, Beliefs, Respect, Need, Want, Support, Achievement

Each phase contains a description of the motivating force behind a wish, how it is reflected in the way a wish is made, and a number of keywords relating to each stage of life. Use these to help confirm the origin of your wish. For instance, if you have discovered that you are asking for something because you seek approval, an adolescence keyword, are you making the wish because you believe it will drastically change your life, an adolescent reflection? Think back to your teenage years and relate your feelings then to your wish now. If you sought approval during those years, how did you feel and how did you gain approval? This energy may still be a part of your life now, and consequently you may hinder your wish by summoning old energy or old ways of being. On the other hand, you may have sought approval during your childhood; allow your creative power to guide you in uncovering motivations and achieving your dearest wishes.

If a keyword is not present, you might notice something else that is familiar about the wish narrative. Notice any resemblances to your life—how your wish is formed, when you want it to manifest, if it is a life-changing wish, how much you crave its manifestation, and so on.

Understanding motivations that are based in one of the life stages will give you the opportunity to filter out superfluous wishes that are no longer relevant, such as wishing for a relationship that was over years ago or wishing for a new car when you already own one. This is not to say that you will not manifest these things if you wish for them. However, it seems pointless to waste energy on wishing for everything that is already in your life or wishing for something from your past when it is time to let go and live in the present.

In the Beginning Was the Wish....

Now you have the basis for designing the right wish for you. This is the beginning. In order to make the right wish, you also need to give it strong foundations. You have discovered that you have the power to create, namely your creative power. You have used this power unconsciously—that is, until now. You learned how to uncover the initial motivation behind your wish by asking why. This led to exposing when and why it originated in the first place. From here, you discovered whether or not your wish was influenced by an unsuccessful phase in your life or if you were making a wish that is no longer relevant, and therefore doomed to failure. Either way, it has been a journey of self-discovery.

If you as an adult want something different, then you need to transform some aspect of yourself and accept a new way of being. Although this will be challenging, it is the only way to go—if you want to create what you most desire in your life. The foundations have been laid. The structure is yet to come.

Here are the main points for building a strong wish sense foundation:

1. Focus. You can manifest your wishes, but first you need to discover what it is you want.
2. How old are you? This is how long you have been making wishes. Establish if you are making a wish based on your current life and needs or if it originates from a previous need or motivation.
3. If your wish does not manifest, redefine the motivation behind the wish, assess if it is a current desire, and design your wish accordingly.

You will learn in your own time how to design the perfect wish for you. The next four chapters will help you to gain better insight into the powers at work in the universe and the laws ruling these powers. They will give you the basis for your mental workout, stretching it beyond its current limit. Bear in mind that you have just begun the process of wish sense. Like anything worth having, practice makes perfect!

WISH PRACTICE:
Dream Path

☆ ★ ☆ ⋆ ☆ ⋆ ☆ ⋆ ★ ☆ ⋆ ☆ ⋆ ☆ ⋆ ★ ☆ ⋆ ☆ ⋆ ☆

Find a picture that speaks to you of who you want to be and what you want to achieve in your life. Place this in the center of a blank piece of paper. Now find some pictures that show each step in achieving your dream life. For example, if you have chosen a picture of a happy family life, the steps to achieve it would probably be a good job, a nice home, a partner, children, money, vacations, and so forth. Take these additional pictures and place them in their natural order—how you would expect to achieve your dream logically. Spiral the pictures around your first picture like a path from the natural beginning to the achievement of your dream. Place this picture in a prominent place somewhere in your home. Look at it regularly and know that all of your wishes can be attained, but just as in life, they have to be reached in degrees.

☆ ★ ★ ★ ☆ ★ ☆ ★ ☆ ★ ★ ★ ☆ ★ ☆ ★ ☆ ★ ★ ★ ☆ ★ ☆ ★ ☆

Pat is a client and single parent who found balancing work and family a challenge. Her wish was for a successful career and a happy home. Pat decided to make a collage of her wish, following the Wish Practice above. Since she had some knowledge of feng shui, she hung the collage in what she knew to be the power place of her home, and then forgot about it. A few months later, a new friend noticed the collage and asked about it. Pat took the collage from the wall and scanned the images she had placed in it. Each image was almost an exact replica of what had occurred in her life since its creation. She realized that her wish had indeed manifested with very little effort on her part. Wish sense can be effortless, and it works.

The Big Picture

Imagine that you are looking closely at a television screen but can see only the dots. The dots do not make any sense until you stand back and view the whole picture. This analogy is similar to how wish sense works. In order to make the right wish, you need to appreciate the greater picture. At a basic level, understanding the motivating force behind your creative power will help you to design the right wish. However, you are a complex individual with a lifetime of experiences, which can either hinder or help the manifestation of your wishes. Experience is the key to consciousness, and knowledge is the key to awareness. Therefore, increasing your knowledge will help you to become more aware of your choices and allow you to create the experience of your heart's desire. In other words, you are learning how to consciously create the life you want!

WISH SENSE TIPS

1. Are you living your dream? Your ability to make your dreams a reality is similar to the way you manifest your wishes.
2. There are no coincidences. These are just points on the compass of your life that help you to know that your creative power is guiding you in the right direction.
3. Sometimes a wish can take a change of focus. Own your creative power!
4. Understand your motivations. This will give you the opportunity to recognize the potential success of a wish and to filter out redundant wishes that are no longer useful. Do you already have what you want? If you do, then wishing for it again might not work. Look at what is behind your wish to help steer you toward your true wish.
5. Notice who is asking for the wish. Is it the adult part of you, the unfulfilled child, or the desire of the adolescent? Once you know who is asking, then you can decide if the wish is really relevant in your life right now.
6. What steps can you take today to achieve your wish? Actor Will Rogers said, "Even if you're on the right track, you'll get run over if you just sit there." Taking a step toward it will help move energy in the direction of your wish.
7. No one said this was going to be easy. Once you make the decision to make changes in your life, stick with it.

Part II
Wishful Thinking

What lies behind us and what lies before us are tiny
matters compared to what lies within us.

—Ralph Waldo Emerson

3

Creating Your Own Reality

It doesn't matter who you are, where you come from.
The ability to triumph begins with you. Always.

—Oprah Winfrey

Most people have heard the phrase "we create our own reality." Essentially, what it means is that we are responsible for everything that happens in our lives, including both the trauma and the joy. This does not necessarily mean that something you did yesterday is going to affect you today. There is much more to this statement, and it is one that is often quoted and yet much misunderstood.

We are response-able for how we respond to the events in our lives. In other words, the events that occur happen because we attract to us something about them that will allow us to respond to them, thereby recognizing more fully who we truly are, what we are capable of, and how we will react in any given situation. We are response-able for our actions—we are able to respond, and this response is how we get to know ourselves better.

Life is complex and simple, all at the same time. We are creative beings who seem to be subconsciously driven to learn more about ourselves. From a human perspective we do not always understand the idea that we would choose to invite pain into our lives. Yet some of the undesired circumstances we create give us an opportunity to choose how we will react or respond—which in turn helps us to learn and grow. It may be that we experience illness or trauma in our lives not only so that we can learn from it but so that others have the opportunity to learn too. Remember, our deepest beliefs influence what we attract to us, regardless of what we think or say we want.

33

There is more about this concept later in the book. For now, realize that while you might create everything in your life, to a large extent what you create is not done so consciously. And this book will help you to understand and use your creative power to become more conscious of what you attract into your life.

Where Attention Goes, Energy Flows

When we break down any object, such as a chair or a body, into smaller and smaller pieces, we eventually arrive at an atom. Breaking down the atom further produces subatomic particles—in other words, matter that is smaller than the atom. One of these subatomic particles is called an electron, or quantum. At the quantum level of matter, the physical world we live in is a mass of energy vibrating at different frequencies. Sometimes the frequency produces a chair; at other times it creates a body.

When matter is perceived at this subatomic level of existence, physicists have discovered that it becomes dimensionless and no longer resembles matter as we know it. This is a difficult concept to grasp because everything around us appears to possess some dimensional form. This branch of science, the study of subatomic particles, is better known as quantum physics.

The saying "where attention goes, energy flows" is particularly relevant in quantum physics. It has been discovered that quantum electrons display a unique chameleon-like ability to appear in one of two forms: as either a particle, which has form, or a wave, which is formless. Interestingly, the only time electrons exist as particles, taking form, is when they are being observed. That is to say, they change form because attention, or the energy of thought, is directed at them. In other words, it has been scientifically proven that thought influences the behavior of matter. In rare cases, certain individuals can essentially create matter—such as the Indian guru Sai Baba, who manifests fragrant oils, vibhuti (sacred ash), and even jewelry. For those of us who are mere dabblers in the quantum realm, just the understanding that our thoughts can and do affect the behavior of matter is enough to stimulate our creative powers for wishing.

Many quantum scientists believe that the universe is made up of these "invisible" quanta, which theoretically means that if we did not exist to "see" the quanta, the world would be a completely different matter. This implies that everything exists in the manner it does because we give it energy; it does not exist independently. If this is correct, then you are the cocreator of everything in existence—proving that you have an unparalleled ability to direct energy. This brings us back to where this started: where attention goes, energy flows. You influence the energetic resonance of your living space, your work environment, and your relationships—you have created your own reality!

Unconscious Thoughts

Thought is probably one of the most powerful energies in the world. Information can be sent or received by a much-misunderstood piece of equipment, the brain. Your mind, which manages all information that passes through the brain, is an enigma, and much of what we do know about how it works is unfathomable. We believe that the most powerful part, the subconscious mind, lies beneath the surface—like an iceberg. The subconscious contains the programs for such things as walking and talking as well as the memory of everything that has ever happened in your life.

The subconscious mind has no concept of time and runs automatically, so that you do not have to constantly think about how to do something that has already been learned. For instance, a typist stores the memory of the keyboard and the ability to type in the subconscious. As a result, when using a computer or typewriter, it is not essential to look at the keys. The learned ability to drive a car, use a knife and fork, or play a musical instrument are all stored in the memory of the subconscious mind. But the subconscious mind has another, even greater talent. It takes things literally. In other words, if you tell it that you can do something, it will believe you, with no questions asked.

If you say to yourself that you are fat, it believes you; if you maintain that you have no money, it believes you; if you claim to be an alien from another planet, it believes you. It cannot and does not discriminate between what is real and what is imagined or between what is a belief and what is the truth. When you consciously repeat thoughts such as, "It's a pain in the neck," or, "I can't stand it," or, "I'm heartbroken," your subconscious mind does not think, "Oh, you are just saying that; you don't really mean it!"

This might not be a problem except that your subconscious mind sets out to create whatever you tell it, and you have told it that this is your reality—at least that is what it hears from your conscious mind. As your servant, the subconscious believes everything you tell it and will give you anything you request. So if you keep saying that you have got a pain in the neck, heartache, or leg problems, then that is exactly what it will create for you, as any good servant would.

This is typically not an overnight occurrence. It can take years to imprint the unconscious with the effect of something said over and over again, and can often depend upon the emotional foundation and intention behind repeated words. Sometimes we only need to repeat something once and it will sink into the subconscious to manifest as reality. Most times, though, it can take longer, much longer. Remember that regardless of the time it takes, thought affects matter and our experience of reality.

This capacity to create a specific outcome using repeated words is also used to bring about positive change. A repeated positive statement, often called an affirmation, acts upon the subconscious mind to initiate change. Using affirmations can be a wonderful way to change negative self-talk. Changing anything can take time on a conscious level, and yet at a quantum level it can happen instantly. So be kind to yourself and believe in your creative power to make positive changes. Abraham Lincoln said, "Most folks are about as happy as they make up their minds to be." Happiness is a decision and so is change.

Picture Perfect

Although focusing your energy on a negative situation will create a challenging outcome, making a statement that uses a negative creates the opposite effect. Your subconscious mind cannot distinguish between positive and negative statements. This is because it works in pictures, and there are no pictures for negative statements, only for positive ones. So, when you say you do not want something in your life, your mind creates the picture of you having it.

For example, if you say that you must not forget something, the picture you will create in your mind is of doing just that, forgetting it! Instead of saying that you will remember something, you have said that you must not forget it. If you take away the negative part of this statement—*not*—then the result is an internal affirmation that says, "I will forget this." Your subconscious mind creates this image, because that is what it heard.

If I said to you, "Don't think of a white polar bear," your subconscious mind has to make a picture of a white polar bear before the conscious mind can try to process the "don't think about it" part. So, making a statement in the negative creates the opposite effect. To remedy this, simply state the positive: "I will remember," or better still, "I am remembering." Using positive statements, you picture what you want to happen.

Thought is creative! Have you ever had the experience of putting on a favorite piece of clothing or white pants and then imagining the worst that can happen, such as spilling the ketchup, and then ... whoops? The top falls off the ketchup bottle and you look like you've just walked off the set of a horror movie. And yet, when you wear old clothes, you manage to keep them spotless. This is probably because you don't care if you spill anything, so you don't make any pictures of doing that, and hence there is no thought or energy attached to ruining the old clothes or getting them dirty.

See how much power you have? If you are good at creating the kinds of situations you don't want, then start to acknowledge just how powerful you are, and begin today to become the conscious creator of your wish-fulfilled life.

Visualization

Visualization is defined as making something visible to one's mind. When you imagine something, you create a picture in your mind, and this image can filter into your everyday life. For instance, if you fear something, then you can tend to repeatedly visualize it occurring in your life, thereby fueling the energy needed to manifest it.

Imagery techniques are well known by athletes to affect their physical performance. Australian psychologist Alan Richardson used basketball players to test the power of visualization. He took three separate groups of players, assigning each the same task to be implemented by a slightly different approach. Members of group one practiced shooting baskets for twenty minutes each day to improve their performance. Group two did nothing—neither practice, nor visualization. Members of group three spent twenty minutes a day visualizing themselves shooting baskets and achieving a 100 percent score.

The results were astonishing. As expected, the basket-shooting ability of group two remained unchanged, group one improved shooting ability by 24 percent, but group three had the most impressive results. Through imagery alone members of this group had increased their basket-shooting ability by 23 percent. This is only 1 percent less than the group that improved their practice through physical effort.

Essentially, they had affected an exclusively physical activity through the power of their own minds. Richardson stated in his paper on the experiment, published in *Research Quarterly*, that the most effective visualization occurs when the person visualizing not only sees an event or situation, but feels it as well. For the basketball players, for instance, this would mean that in addition to imagining the ball going through the hoop, they would have to feel the ball in their hands, hear it bouncing on the floor, and experience the feeling of elation when they scored.

The ability to influence matter is not just confined to humans. René Peoc'h, in association with the Swiss Foundation Marcel et Monique Odier de Psycho-Physique, performed an experiment using a robot called a tychoscope and a cage full of live chicks. He used two groups of chicks: one group was imprinted with the robot as a maternal substitute, while the other group that did not imprint was placed in a darkened room with a candle on the robot. When the robot was allowed to roam freely within each cage on its own, it would randomly move between the left and right side equally. However, once either of the groups of chicks was placed on one side of the cage, the tychoscope's pattern changed. It spent more time on the side with the chicks. It appeared that the chicks were willing the robot to stay with them. It was concluded that the imprinted chicks may have wanted to be close to what they assumed was their mother, and that the other chicks might have wanted the robot to stay near because they did not like the dark. Either way, it would seem that the chicks were influencing matter.

Physicist Helmut Schmidt, author of *Psychic Exploration: A Challenge for Science*, performed a similar experiment involving a cat and a heat lamp. He linked up the heat lamp to a machine that would randomly switch it on and off. As expected, the amount of time the lamp was turned on equaled the time it was turned off during its random activity. Then the cat was placed in front of the heat lamp during cold weather. This time the results showed that the heat lamp was on more than it was off. The likelihood of the cat imagining itself curled up in front of a cozy, hot fire, sensing how much nicer it would be to stay warm, is not beyond all possibility. Or the cat may have desired the feeling of being warm, and this feeling was linked to its internal image of the heat lamp. The control had shown that the equipment was performing accurately, and therefore, the only explanation was that somehow the cat was influencing the heat lamp. Its thoughts manipulated a physical object to create a comfortable reality. If a cat or a cage full of chicks can do this, just imagine what you can do!

In order to visualize constructively, it is essential to be familiar with the following guidelines:

1. Build your visualization image. Construct your image so it is as real as possible. For instance, if your wish is for a house, where is it located, what does it look like, how many rooms

does it have, what are the grounds around it like, what color is the front door, and so on?

2. Visualize something that invokes enthusiasm. Your image should create excitement when you visualize it. For example, imagine you are a tennis player and your visualization is to be the best in the world. For a tennis player this would conjure up excitement, but for someone with little interest in the sport it would be wasted energy. Think of something that makes you feel exhilarated, and remember this feeling when you visualize. If you are excited about something, this increases the dynamic, and your wish is more likely to be created in your reality.

3. Include yourself. Always picture yourself in the image. If you want a new job, imagine yourself with the job. If you wish for a house, visualize yourself in the house. If you wish for something less tangible such as peace of mind, or wisdom, imagine yourself in a situation that you associate with this quality. If you wish for peace, visualize yourself in a garden with only the sound of nature as your companion. If you desire wisdom, create in your mind's eye a picture of yourself imparting wisdom to a group of avid listeners, or envision yourself as all-knowing. Once you have pictured a desired outcome, let the image go so that your subconscious mind can move toward your wish.

Visualization is an invaluable creative tool. In addition to its use as an instrument for manifestation, it can also be utilized to change some aspect of your life that is not working for you. For instance, if you do not have enough money, visualize a cash machine giving you lots of money, or imagine receiving a bank statement indicating that you have plenty of money in your account.

Mental Magnetism

Your mind is a magnetic instrument that sends messages via electrical impulses; it will attract to it the energy of your most predominant thoughts. By focusing on something, you unconsciously move toward it. Most people place the mind exclusively within the brain. Yet research shows that the mind can be located in other areas of the body as well. It appears to be stored both inside every cell of the body and within the electromagnetic field surrounding each living being. This means that your thoughts, which are energy, could be likened to a calling card, because your entire energy field extends beyond your being. This principle of attraction explains all those situations you wished for, as well as those you said you never wanted. Imagine what you could do if you focused and visualized all your energy into wanting something good in your life. We've all heard the saying "the sky's the limit," but it really is limitless for you because you are full of boundless energy and infinite possibilities.

Positive Thought and Negative Programming

Just as you exercise your body, you also need to exercise your mind to make it fit and healthy. In order for you to achieve wish sense thoughts, you will want to reprogram your mind so it can work to your advantage. Changing what has already been learned can be challenging, but it is possible. Imagine that your mind is a computer; all you have to do to change the program is remove the disc and replace it with a new one containing only positive phrases and words of encouragement. Sounds easy enough, doesn't it?

Consider the familiar question, "Is the glass half empty, or is the glass half full?" Declaring the glass to be half empty denotes a negative outlook, while stating that the glass is half full signifies a positive attitude. When we practice wish sense, we want to summon all of our creative power, including choosing to use positive words to support our wishes coming true. Remember Muhammad Ali, the former world heavyweight champion, whose motto was that he was "The Greatest"? He believed it, and if he didn't accept it as true at the beginning of his career, he kept on saying it until it became true for him and for all of his fans too!

41

If, as another example, you have a challenge receiving gifts or acts of kindness, you might affirm, "I am ready to receive my wish with open arms and an open heart." This has a different energy from, "I am willing to be open to the manifestation of my wishes." Each word is an ingredient that adds a different flavor, so use words that will leave a sweet taste in your mouth.

Use words that are attractive to you and engage your passion. For example, if you want to change your appearance by losing weight, you might say, "The pounds are falling off as I accomplish my ideal weight." Or, consider how much more effective it would be if you said, "I look stunning and feel magnificent as I realize my ideal weight." In addition to being positive and encouraging, this second affirmation not only contains more energy than the first statement, but it also gives a visually tantalizing image of how you can look and feel during this change. This will improve your chances of manifesting your dreams because it puts your heart into the mix. All affirmations are created in present tense. The same goes for your wish. Keep it in the present moment and not in the future.

It is important to remember that your creative power is about you. It should not be used to try to change someone else's reality. If someone treats you inappropriately and you feel wronged, remember that nobody has the ability to oppress you until you give them permission. This does not mean that you would consciously consent to being badly treated. On the contrary, it is more likely that if you are feeling oppressed there is a deep-seated belief that allows this behavior; on some level you might believe that you don't deserve any better. In order to activate change around something like this, create an internal reality that transforms the way you feel about yourself—using, among other tools, positive words and thoughts. This will in turn create a new external reality for you and alter the way others respond to you.

We often use negative statements to express the way we are feeling about something and do not realize the damaging impact they can have on our lives. For instance, if you dislike your job, the repeated negative statement in your mind might be, "I hate my job." This acts like an affirmation too. Since your subconscious mind works in pictures, the picture you create will be of a job you hate. This vision imprisons you in an unhappy situation. If you were to change this statement to, "I am ready to accept a new job," or, "I am open to receive an offer of a wonderful new job now," you create a new picture of something that you want in your life. On the other hand, if you say to yourself, "I love and accept all the wonderful opportunities my job offers me," the job you already have might undergo a transformation and suddenly become the perfect job.

Using negative words binds you to the detrimental energy associated with them, whereas positive language and expressions promote a more promising response. For instance, consider the following words: *love, hate, joy,* and *pain.* What immediately comes to mind as you say those words? What images are conjured up as you read each one separately? Words have either been formed from our internal images or they evoke an internal image; either way, picturing or visualizing creates your experience of reality on some level. This is why it is so important to be consciously aware of the words you are using when you communicate. Positive words create positive pictures, and negative words create negative ones. Wishing is a positive experience, so be kind to yourself as you imagine and express what you want.

Successful wish sense invokes the power of positive words, so if you want something, be mindful of your language. Well-known diarist Anaïs Nin said, "We don't see things as they are; we see them as we are." Changing the way you speak to yourself and how you express yourself to others will alter your experience of life.

Have you noticed that when you start your day in a positive frame of mind, the remainder is usually more pleasant? Purposefully creating your day will make it more enjoyable and attract an abundance of positive energy into your life. Positive words have a deep impact on our being, more than we could imagine.

Dr. Masaru Emoto's book *The Hidden Messages of Water* illustrates the influence our words and feelings have on water molecules. The book is packed with photographs of water molecules that go from looking aesthetically beautiful when positive and harmonious words and feelings are directed at them, to appearing discordant and misshapen when negative words and feelings are aimed toward them. If these energies are present in water molecules, and the human body is 70 percent water, then what do you imagine your body looks like when your mind and emotions relay positive or negative words and feelings to it?

For a moment, close your eyes and imagine the following words one by one. Try to get a sense of each word's intention and feeling. Spend time thinking about everything associated with each word: love, hate, happiness, sadness, birth, death, blocked, free, music, silence. You may discover positive and negative feelings attached to each word, but for the most part I expect that you will resonate with their true meaning.

I use an exercise in my workshops to demonstrate the power of positive thinking. It is an effective way of visually showing people how negative and positive thoughts affect the physical body. It takes about one minute to do and emphasizes the instantaneous response that the physical body has to our thoughts. I ask someone from the group who is physically fit to stand up and think of something that makes him or her feel negative, such as a situation that might invoke unhappy, sad, or angry feelings. Once this feeling is assimilated, the student raises the dominant arm at a right angle to the side of the body and resists me as I gently push down on the arm.

The dominant arm would normally be the strongest, but what happens is that the negative thoughts and feelings weaken the energy and the arm instantly falls back to the side. The student then invokes positive thoughts and feelings, raising the nondominant arm and ready to resist pressure I exert on it. This time the response is startling. He or she can be so strong that I could in some instances swing on the arm. This goes to prove that in a matter of moments your thoughts, positive or negative, can have a significant influence on your physical well-being. Think what kind of impact a sustained thought could have.

Create an Inspirational Day

Now that you know how positive and negative words affect you, make a date with yourself to spend the day in a conscious way. First, decide which day of the week is going to be your positive-thoughts day. Make a note on your calendar that on this day you will only think, say, and embody positive energy. Inform your family, friends, and work colleagues about your decision and ask them if they would like to join you in this pursuit. Make a list of positive actions you can take during this day. For instance, you could give someone a compliment every hour on the hour. If you decide to do this, make sure to include yourself because you deserve to be praised too. If you read magazines, choose articles with upbeat story lines. The same goes for any radio or television programs you tune in to. Try to find shows that inspire you and make you happy. At the end of your positive day, make a note of how you feel emotionally, physically, mentally, and spiritually.

Here are some other wish sense tips to get you going:

1. Be aware of your use of negative or challenging expressions and change them as often as you possibly can to positive expressions of truth.
2. Think only the best of people and situations.
3. Be mindful of gossip, and resolve to omit unkind words from your language.
4. Be considerate not only of others but also of yourself.
5. Take a look in the mirror and begin today to say nice things about yourself. Saying phrases such as "I am gorgeous" or "I love you" and really meaning them will alter your whole way of being, creating an abundance of positive energy all around you. To start with, your conscious mind may not believe you, but your subconscious is listening and believes every word you say.

Altering your language will have a profound impact on your life. Just loving yourself creates a wonderful new and powerful energy.

You need to be willing to exchange old ways of being for a new reality. If telling yourself that you are gorgeous or loving yourself is beyond your capability, then change the way you feel about yourself by degrees. If you are unable to say "I love you," begin by saying "I accept myself as I am" followed by "I am worthy of love" and finally "I love you." Go through as many levels as you need—whatever works for you. Eventually, these truths will filter through to your conscious mind and your life will begin to change.

Believe It or Not

Successful wish sense begins with changing negative thought patterns. The Swiss psychiatrist Carl Jung said, "When an inner situation is not made conscious, it appears outside as fate." What limits you is your belief in limitation. If you have always believed that life is hard, then fate will allow you to follow this concept by presenting you with choices that continue to fuel your belief. Hence, your life stays the same. Remember, the subconscious mind is your servant. Not only will it attract your most predominant thoughts, but also your strongest beliefs. What you think superficially does not have to be true; it is what you believe at a deep level that is most important when it comes to creating your reality.

For instance, a client recently had an ah-ha moment during one of our sessions together. She wanted to write a book, and yet every time she tried to start writing she developed writer's block and froze up, or something occurred in her life that put the writing on hold. As a consciously aware psychotherapist, she understood the patterns of the psyche yet had not linked her writer's block with the abusive behavior she had suffered in the past at the hands of both her father and husband.

She had already gone through much change to become a therapist. This was in part reflected by her ability to have a healthy and loving relationship with a new partner. Although the cruelty she suffered and the subsequent belief patterns it invoked had been healed at the relationship level, it still lurked in her subconscious and was now threatening her creativity. It transpired that her feelings of not being worthy now emerged in her life in the guise of not having something worth sharing with others.

Once she realized that this old pattern was affecting her writing career, she made an intention to change the belief. She did this by meditating in front of the computer before writing anything, including emails. The focus of her meditation was directed toward positive affirmations of her worthiness to share her knowledge. Just affirming that she was a great teacher was not enough. She also realized that she needed to include her acceptance of the recognition this would entail. This opened up a completely new world for her, and she was able to slowly but surely progress as a writer.

Everything in your life will mirror your beliefs, and repeated patterns of events, thoughts, or circumstances are clues to the beliefs you hold dear. From the moment we are born we begin to form thought patterns. As the name suggests, a pattern or neural pathway follows the same lines again and again. Patterns are ideas and experiences that create blueprints for our behavior. Neural pathways or behavioral patterns are established in the basal ganglia, a part of the brain that is significant in habits, addictions, and procedural learning, such as riding a bike or driving a car.

From the moment a pattern is imprinted into the neural pathways, everything that your mind associates with that idea or belief is modeled on the same pattern. Similarly, you create your reality first in your mind and then in the world you live in. It sounds simple, but becomes more complicated when you appreciate that your reality is also influenced by a combination of your beliefs, expectations, fears, and past experiences. These influences have already created the patterns in your life. So every time you make a wish, you unconsciously base its creation on an available pattern in your mind. As a result, your wish manifests in a pattern that is familiar, although this particular pattern may not be what you really want. Consequently, some wishes appear to go unrealized and yet, upon closer inspection, they might have manifested through the familiar route of an established pattern. What do you do? Simply change the original pattern.

Some habit patterns are beneficial, such as brushing your teeth or saying please and thank you. Some patterns mirror your experience of the world you live in and can create positive or detrimental habits. They can develop in every life situation, often showing up as the same scenario, but as in a movie remake, the people and the scenery change. Your awareness of repeated situations that you no longer wish to experience offers you the opportunity to change the pattern.

For example, a friend of mine was unhappy in her job. She was having some personality conflicts with her boss and she was not getting the recognition that she felt she deserved. She had similar problems in her relationships with her neighbors. Eventually, she made the decision to leave her job and change her residence, thinking this would put an end to her unhappiness. Her next job lasted for a year and ended due to continued personality conflicts with her boss and lack of recognition. She relocated again for the same reasons as before!

This went on for several years until she finally figured out that instead of looking outside herself, it was time to look within. After all, she was the common thread in her unhappiness. She realized that she had chosen to stay in situations that were neither nurturing nor successful because she believed, on some level, that she was not good enough to do the job she really wanted to do. This belief played out in both her work and home environments and was constantly reflected by others not respecting her needs. Yet the truth of the matter was that she was not respecting her own needs.

You may have noticed a similar scenario playing out in your own life. Although my friend continually manifested her wish for a new job and home, it was not until she changed something within her that she achieved the peace she wanted. The manifestation of her ultimate wish resulted in a career that confirmed her talents and a home she loved.

Sometimes, however, your patterns run a little deeper, meaning that you are oblivious to the root cause of your actions. As the saying goes, "old habits die hard." Let's say that you are constantly in debt, so you make a wish for more money. Despite this, no matter how hard you try to save money, it just keeps slipping through your fingers. You employ an accountant to help change this pattern, yet it appears that you are fighting a losing battle as money continues to disappear at an alarming speed.

This pattern could stem from an inner belief that you do not deserve to have money, or that money is the root of all evil and you have to get rid of it as soon as possible. Maybe you harbor the belief that life is a struggle, and this is the way it is supposed to be. If you had money you would not be able to support this deeper and unconscious belief. Instead, you create situations to prevent yourself from retaining money, such as untimely bills and unforeseen expenses, allowing your belief in struggle to continue.

Alternatively, the belief might have originated from one of your family members, a peer group, the media, or school and you embraced it as your own belief. In any case, it is something you are familiar with, and therefore tends to repeat itself as a pattern in your life. The reasons can be close to the surface, but generally unwanted patterns show up because they are based on hidden or unexamined beliefs. To change a habit you need to confront your patterns, recognize how they evolved, and be willing to change them.

Unwanted patterns can block your ability to manifest your wishes, especially patterns concerning self-worth and self-esteem. You stand a much better chance of manifesting your wish by believing that you deserve to receive it. Becoming consciously aware of your patterns and being willing to change them will help to transform your life. If you are reluctant to take responsibility for your choices, it is likely that you will continue to create the same unhappy situations in your life.

When you make the decision to change an unwanted pattern, you will notice that events occur to challenge your new beliefs. Just the decision to change this pattern may actually energize it, since it is something that you are focusing on.

For instance, let's say you are constantly attracted to men or women who are unfaithful to you. Tired of this kind of relationship, you resolve to exit the dating scene. Almost at the same moment you make this decision, your best friend sets you up on a blind date.

According to your friend, this person has never been unfaithful, so you agree to try once more. So far, so good!

The "unfaithful" challenge may arise in a different way, however. Perhaps he or she has a dependent to care for and so a three-way relationship occurs again, but in a different form ... or the person is career oriented and does not have time to concentrate on a committed partnership, the career being the other factor in the three-way ... or he or she is going through a divorce and you end up being the rebound relationship. Making the decision to change this energy by forging an intention to only attract someone who is faithful and available can sometimes be the pattern breaker.

Alas, getting to this point can often take a little effort, especially if the undesirable pattern relates to painful circumstances that have yet to be healed, such as parents divorcing or the loss of a close family member at an early age. These events can produce the kind of pain that the inner self wishes to avoid. So in this example, a pattern of unsuccessful relationships prevents you from having to experience a deeper loss. Of course, this is just a delusion, an unconscious way of avoiding painful circumstances that, in the long run, inhibits us from fulfilling our true wishes.

Other challenges can be quite straightforward. For example, have you noticed that when you go on a diet you receive an abundance of invitations to go out to dinner? Or the minute you clear out the wardrobe of all your 1970s clothing, your best friend has a 1970s theme party?

Undesirable patterns are there for a reason. They unconsciously serve you by protecting you from knowing how powerful you are, how powerful you can be. Marianne Williamson, author of *A Return to Love*, says in one of her most famous quotes, "There is nothing enlightened about shrinking so that other people won't feel insecure around you." By keeping yourself small, you may be protecting others so that they can live with their limitations.

Take a moment now to think of a pattern of behavior that has prevented you from achieving your wish or has stopped you from having something in your life that you most wanted. Ask yourself these questions:

"What does the continuation of this (unwanted) behavior allow me to gain?"

"What am I avoiding because of this pattern?"

"What is the purpose of this pattern in my life?"

Television psychologist Dr. Phil McGraw says that you cannot change what you do not acknowledge. The first step in breaking a pattern is recognition; the second is your willingness to transform old patterns or old beliefs. Being aware of the choices your subconscious is making will help you to select options that serve you. To do this you can simply say to yourself, "I am free of this belief, and I now choose to believe that . . ." Or, if you are unaware of the belief pattern that creates the outcome, ask yourself, "What do I believe about myself in order for this situation to have occurred?"

Be prepared to have your resolve tested. You can take definitive action to change, but when you want to transform unfavorable patterns and beliefs, you will need perseverance to face the challenges your decision will present in your life. However, if you are really serious about wanting to make your wishes come true, then you will find the strength to see your resolutions through. Author and speaker Dr. Wayne Dyer says, "When you change the way you look at things, then the things you look at change."

WISH PRACTICE:
If I Only Knew. . .

☆ ⋆ ★ ⋆ ☆ ⋆ ☆ ⋆ ☆ ⋆ ★ ⋆ ☆ ⋆ ☆ ⋆ ☆ ⋆ ★ ⋆ ☆ ⋆ ☆ ⋆ ☆

You can use a question-and-answer technique similar to the Why exercise in chapter 2 to establish where a pattern originated.

First, find a comfortable position, close your eyes, and relax. When you feel ready, ask yourself a series of questions:

1. If I knew how old I was when this pattern was first created, how old would I have been?

2. If I knew who else was involved when this pattern was first created, who would it have been?
3. If I knew why I created this pattern, why did I create it?
4. If I knew what beliefs I created because of this situation or event, what beliefs would they be?

Allow the thoughts connected with each question to just flow through your mind without judgment. In other words, do not think too much about the answer.

If this exercise does not work for you, then the Stepping Out meditation in chapter 4 will help you to discover where your patterns originated and offer a model to facilitate change. Also, the exercise of writing with your nondominant hand described in chapter 2 may be a helpful tool for you to use to determine the source of your patterns. Adapt the questions to uncover the answers you need. Be gentle with yourself. It takes time to change a pattern. Identifying the pattern is half the equation, so in essence, once you recognize what needs to be healed you are already halfway to healing it.

☆ ★ ★ ☆ ★ ☆ ★ ☆ ★ ★ ★ ☆ ★ ☆ ★ ☆ ★ ★ ★ ☆ ★ ☆ ★ ☆

Role-Playing

Of course, you can take things a step further and literally create your reality by becoming what you most want to attract. One way to do this is to "fake it till you make it!" Sometimes this can help you to recognize whether you really want something to be a part of your life. For example, if your greatest wish is to become a movie star, then bring this energy into your life by acting like one. Embody the kind of qualities you admire in a star of your choice. Get in some practice, see how it feels, own the space, wear the suit—be what you always wanted to be. There is no point staying at home waiting to be discovered. No one is going to discover you until you discover yourself. Once you recognize your talents and abilities, you allow others to do the same. Your recognition creates an energy that makes the rest of the world sit up and take notice. Then you will no longer have to fake it because it will already be a part of your reality.

The self-images you project determine how others see you. Trust that you can create whatever you want in your life. Let go of the roles that no longer serve you and accept a new part to play, one that fully expresses who you want to be and how you want to feel. Know without a doubt that you create your life, so you may as well create that wonderful job, home, or relationship you want. You will get from life what you expect to get, and the same goes for making wishes come true. There are universal laws of attraction at work helping you to achieve your wish, assisting you with the creation of your heart's desires. If you do not believe it will happen, then you will be right, because it won't. In the book *The Alchemist*, a fable about following one's dream, author Paulo Coelho asserts, "When you want something, all the universe conspires in helping you to achieve it."

We sometimes associate who we are with characters from books, films, or fairy tales, or with real people who have lived through specific eras, or even with songs. I have always loved Jane Austen's book *Pride and Prejudice* and considered that I have very similar qualities to the main character and my namesake, Elizabeth Bennet, such as her independence and how she sticks to her values and lives by her own standards, not society's. From a young age, I also associated with writer Emily Brontë, author of *Wuthering Heights*. I felt the tragedy of her life, her pain, and her emotional instability as something that reflected my earlier life, while her passion for the Yorkshire moors mirrored my own infatuation with this barren land.

WISH PRACTICE:
Role-Playing Roles

✰ ★ ★ ☆ ・ ☆ ・ ☆ ★ ☆ ・ ☆ ・ ☆ ★ ☆ ・ ☆ ・ ☆

For this exercise, take a piece of paper, write your name at the top, and use the questions below to help you to access your story, character, and the role you are playing in this life at this moment. Note the realizations you gain by answering the questions.

1. Is there a character, fictional or nonfictional, that you admire and associate with or who has had an impact on your life?
2. What is it about this person that makes an impact on you?
3. Which positive and negative qualities do you embody that are personified by this person?
4. If your life were a book, movie, fairy tale, or song, which one would it be? If one does not come to mind, then make up a title for your life.
5. What is it about that book, movie, fairy tale, or song that affects you?

Look back at the responses you gave and see how much of yourself you can see in the stories you like and the characters you admire. Do their qualities get in the way of them achieving their dreams? Are these same qualities stopping your dreams from coming true?

Now think of a positive, upbeat story with a happy ending. What is different about this story and the characters in it, in comparison to the ones you chose for your life? Are they more optimistic? Did they get everything they wanted in the story?

Finally, write a short story about your life, only bringing positive qualities into it. Include the positive aspects of the information that you have received so far during this exercise. Illustrate the positive qualities of the characters you admire and the story lines or theme songs that touched you, but make them all about you. Imagine that this story also contains the manifestation of your wish. How would the story end? How would the hero/heroine feel at the end of the story?

Alternatively, you can think of someone with qualities that you would like to embody and imagine that you are standing in their shoes. How does it feel to be this person? Maybe for one day, imagine that you are this person; dress the part, act the role—how would you spend your day?

This exercise can help you to appreciate the kind of energy you are putting into your life and the expectations you have for a positive outcome of your wishes.

✫ ⋆ ★ ⋆ ✫ ⋆ ✫ ⋆ ✫ ⋆ ★ ⋆ ✫ ⋆ ✫ ⋆ ✫ ⋆ ★ ⋆ ✫ ⋆ ✫ ⋆ ✫

Recognize Your Ability to Manifest

We are continually making wishes. Some fail to manifest, yet those with enough feeling behind them often become reality, including the things we do not want.

Take a moment now to consider the following questions. Think of something that you really did not want; you did not ask for it, yet it manifested anyway. When you decided that you did not want this in your life, how did you feel in that moment? Do you remember if you did anything differently? Did you put more energy behind not wanting something and it materializing than behind something you did want and it not manifesting?

The force behind your desire, whether for something you want or do not want, is your passion. Your passion is an intense emotional energy that often has a great deal of enthusiasm behind it. Being passionate means that there might be more intense feelings or emotions connected with not wanting something than with wanting it.

Sometimes we make wishes and then put them at the back of our minds, forgotten and ostensibly unfulfilled. Time passes and suddenly, out of the blue, an old wish materializes. Has this happened to you? Do you remember an instance when a wish you had made and forgotten unexpectedly materialized? Some of these wishes manifest immediately, while others can take years.

I recently spoke to a man who for twenty-five years drove back and forth past his dream house. Then one day his ideal home came on the market. Everything worked out perfectly to enable him to sell his existing home and move into his dream home. It may seem like a coincidence or luck, but his wish manifested at the right time when he could afford it and just when he was able to move in. How long did it take some of your wishes to manifest? Did you still want them to be a part of your life, or were they no longer relevant?

Things I have been passionate about not wanting invariably materialize. Passion creates, and does not distinguish between whether or not the creation is welcome. Pay attention to the similarities in your ability to manifest both positive and negative outcomes. These similarities are the clue to your unique talent. Once you recognize them, you will be able to devote your energy to manifesting the things you want in your life.

WISH SENSE TIPS

1. Visualize what you want rather than what you do not want in your life. Thought is creative, so create a picture in your mind of the desired result.

2. Make all of your expressions positive. It has been discovered that optimists live nineteen percent longer than pessimists, so it is worth looking on the bright side of life.

3. Use positive rather than negative words. As Bing Crosby, well-known singer and star of the movie *White Christmas*, expresses in one of his songs, "Accentuate the positive, eliminate the negative."

4. Recognize the patterns in your life. What do you have to gain by continuing this behavior? If you think a pattern will prevent you from achieving your wish, take steps to transform it.

5. Fake it till you make it. Act like it is already yours.

We create our own reality. Look at what you have consistently created in your life so far. If your thought is so powerful, then why not put it to good use and create what you want in your life instead of what you do not want? If there is something that is not working, there is no point looking outside of yourself. Look no further than within—it is the place where all the answers can be found. Your beliefs, behavioral patterns, the way you think and speak, the roles you play, and even your imagination combine to create the whole package of your life. Although you are the most powerful person in your life, and you know yourself best, sometimes other people can recognize your patterns sooner than you can. Listen to the perspectives of others. You do not have to believe them; just be open to the possibilities. It may take a little time and concentrated effort to decipher the language of a pattern, especially if you are a novice, but in the end it will be worth it.

4

The Fear of Getting
What You Want

**Taking a new step, uttering a new word,
is what people fear most.**

—Fyodor Dostoyevsky

It was only recently that I realized just how resistant I had been to receiving my heartfelt wish. I had wanted something for most of my life and was at a loss to understand why it had not yet manifested. And then quite by accident—or should I say coincidence?—I had a revelation. I could not actualize any of my wishes until I stopped fearing the potential loss of a manifested wish. On the one hand I was making a wish, yet on the other I was preventing its manifestation because I feared losing what I had most dreamt of having. This fear negated all of my wishes.

Fear is your greatest enemy. You can make as many wishes as you like, but your fear will block you like a sixty-foot wall and prevent you from receiving something that is so ready to be yours. We fear so many things, and yet the majority of the time we are completely unaware of our reactions of fear. We fear not having the opportunity to shine, but when the occasion arises, we retreat with the excuse that we are not ready yet. Sometimes we fear life just as much as we fear death. We reject relationships, jobs, lovers, or any situation where we might be challenged to take a risk and choose between success and failure. If we do not make any attempt to try, then we can just talk about the possibility, remaining in the safe confines of the if-only syndrome where hope is less dangerous than actualizing our wishes and dreams.

Changing Beliefs

We have been trained for most of our lives to fear. As children we were taught not to talk to strangers, to be careful on the roads, to speak only when spoken to, to keep our clothes clean, and so on and so forth. This infusion of fear into our tiny little minds was our normal way of life.

From the moment you were born, you have been subjected to the external world. You were an empty vessel that would be filled with the beliefs of those around you. The beliefs and attitudes of your parents, relatives, friends, peers, television, religion, and politics have influenced and molded you into the person you are now. When you were a child, this programming entered your subconscious, and once internalized, became your own. Others' beliefs became your beliefs, their fears your fears. You lacked the experience necessary to distinguish between beliefs that served you and those that were harmful. The unsuccessful aspects of your day-to-day existence primarily originate from negative or challenging belief systems that you continue to harbor. They show up in your relationships, career, home, and bank balance, and will remain intact until you make the decision to change them.

The next meditation will support you in identifying the underlying reasons for challenging beliefs associated with the disappointing areas of your life. Meditation allows you to directly experience your true nature. It is an uninterrupted flow of peace, often achieved through the daily practice of focusing on the breath, calming the emotions, and reducing the activity of the brain. In the Western world we use other methods to attain peace of mind, such as sitting in the garden, walking in the woods, reading, or listening to music. Swami Vivekananda, one of the first Eastern ascetics to introduce meditation to the West, commented that it should be as much a part of life as breathing. In his discourse on meditation he compared thoughts to ripples on a lake and added, "It is only possible for us to catch a glimpse of the bottom when the ripples have subsided, and the water is calm."

Finding the original source of stress will allow more abundance into your life on every level. Decide which aspect of your life you want to concentrate on before going into the meditation. For instance, if you have had a series of unsuccessful relationships, this may be an area worth investigating. Or if you have difficulty retaining money and you are tired of living with a poverty consciousness, this might be a matter requiring some attention.

The following instructions apply to every meditation you carry out. Before you begin any meditation, allocate yourself the free time. Allowing yourself uninterrupted time devoted to your personal development demonstrates how much you value yourself and your growth. Turn off the telephone and close the door to potential disturbances. When you have finished the exercise, drink plenty of water to flush away any built-up emotional toxins.

WISH PRACTICE:
Stepping Out Meditation

☆ ⋆ ★ ⋆ ☆ ⋆ ☆ ⋆ ☆ ⋆ ★ ⋆ ☆ ⋆ ☆ ⋆ ☆ ⋆ ★ ⋆ ☆ ⋆ ☆ ⋆ ☆

Take at least fifteen minutes for this exercise. Find a place free from noise and distractions, lie or sit in a comfortable position with your arms and legs uncrossed, and begin to relax. Close your eyes, calm your mind, and focus your attention on your breathing, releasing any tension by breathing into it . . . if you have difficulty calming your mind, acknowledge your thoughts and let them go; then focus your mind on your breath. Give yourself permission to experience the luxury of complete relaxation.

When you are ready, begin to visualize yourself stepping out of your body and freeing yourself from the confines of the physical world . . . really get a sense of liberation as you stand back from your body . . . see yourself as you are now, surrounded by an egg-shaped beautiful white light, connected by a golden umbilical cord to your body.

Now focus your attention and begin to observe your life as a third party would. Ask in your mind to be shown the first time you played out this unsuccessful aspect of your life. You may receive this information through pictures, thoughts, or feelings. If you do not connect with anything recognizable, either ask again or say to yourself, "If I knew, what would it be?" This is a simple way of accessing an answer without being too attached to the result. Do not doubt that, on some level, you are receiving the answer to your question. Take your time to do this, but do not dwell on any judgments or feelings associated with this situation.

Once you have acknowledged the time when you started to act out this belief, shift your concentration to discovering the initial source and ask in your mind to be shown the circumstances. The belief could have come from someone you knew, from a decision you made when something happened to you, or even from something you read. It is important not to judge any of the information you receive; be open to all the possibilities.

Now that you are aware of when the event first occurred, visualize the incident as it happened. Create the scene in your mind, remembering to include all the details. Once you have done this, you can do one of two things to change the scene:

1. Step back into your body and, by using your imagination, change the circumstances by replacing the image with a positive experience, and then allow this energy to filter through to your present consciousness.
2. Remain as you are, separate from your body, and discuss with the past you how to change the event. Imagine the scene frozen in time like a frame in a movie reel. When you have both decided how best to do this, you can lend your support and love to the past you while assisting in the process of changing the experience.

If you are inspired to use a different technique, do whatever feels right for you. I recommend repeating this meditation until you are completely satisfied that you have successfully initiated change. Take as much time as you need to create a new reality.

When you have finished, bring yourself back to conscious reality. Step back into your body and visualize a spotlight above your head, showering light through your whole being, cleansing your mind, body, and spirit with light. Take some deep breaths and begin to move your arms and legs. When you are ready, open your eyes.

Record the whole meditation, as you experienced it, in your wish journal. This will assist you in remembering all the details, including your insights. Making a decision to change past beliefs will affect your current life in a profound way. Imagine your life is a ten-track music CD. Each decade of your life is reflected by one of the tracks on the CD. This means that in order for you to take a glimpse of your future, all you have to do is skip a few tracks ahead; if you want to review your past, simply play previous tracks. This also means that if you do not like the program, you can change the CD. Be aware that you have energetically altered your history; you have changed your CD and thus may experience reverberations in other areas of your life. It might take time for your new decision to affect your life, or it could be instantaneous.

☆ ★ ★ ★ ☆ ★ ☆ ★ ☆ ★ ★ ★ ☆ ★ ☆ ★ ☆ ★ ★ ★ ☆ ★ ☆ ★ ☆

Meditation can reveal answers that the conscious mind resists—as a client, Mary, discovered during the Stepping Out meditation. Coming from a strict and conservative Irish Catholic background, she could not openly discuss meditation or wish sense with her family. Her father and grandfather were both hard workers and drilled into her that struggling was the only way to survive. But Mary wanted a different life. Of course, it would seem obvious that her inability to manifest abundance stems from her familial background.

Yet her meditation revealed an even bigger influence on her beliefs. It was the religious conditioning she had received as a child. She was told that money was the "root of all evil" and that the only way to be happy was to walk the path of suffering. As a child she took this message to mean that if she became abundantly wealthy, she would be evil and therefore cast out of her church and her family. Just her awareness of the origin of her lack of abundance changed the energy and lifted the belief that was blocking the path to the fulfillment of her wish. This allowed her to receive the gift that had been missing in her life.

Resistance

Change is a major decision. On some level we are all afraid of change because it takes us out of our comfort zone and into a very uncomfortable place where we have to face the truth of who we are. By making a wish, you are asking for some aspect of your life to transform. If you are not prepared for this, then your wish will have to wait until you are ready for it.

WISH PRACTICE:
Change

☆ ★ ★ ☆ ★ ☆ ★ ☆ ★ ★ ★ ☆ ★ ☆ ★ ☆ ★ ★ ★ ☆ ★ ☆

Take a pen and a piece of paper, find a comfortable position, close your eyes, and center yourself for a moment. Centering yourself means finding your place of peace or balance. Once you feel relaxed, open your eyes and think carefully about these next three questions. Going over the questions one at a time, write down any feelings, ideas, thoughts, or images that come to you as you contemplate the answers.

1. If you had what you most wanted in your life, what would it change?
2. Are you ready for your deepest wish to come true?

3. If someone said to you, "By this time tomorrow, your wish will be a reality," how would you feel about that? Does it frighten you?

Your answers to the questions above might reveal some fear and resistance to change. Louise L. Hay, author of *You Can Heal Your Life*, declares, "Some people would rather leave the planet than change." Change is scary, and yet we are continually confronted by it. When people try to transform their outdated beliefs, they act like addicts. This is not necessarily because they think their ideas are right, but because they are addicted to a way of being, and changing this is frightening. Author and philosopher Henry David Thoreau said, "Things do not change, we change." Changing aspects of ourselves that do not work for us will undoubtedly change the people around us as well as the world we live in.

☆ ★ ★ ★ ☆ ・ ☆ ・ ☆ ★ ★ ★ ☆ ・ ☆ ・ ☆ ★ ★ ★ ☆ ・ ☆ ・ ☆

Resistance to change is one of the main reasons wishes do not manifest. Begin to recognize what kind of change-resisting strategies you use: changing the subject, illness, procrastination, daydreaming, creating obstacles, refusing to begin something because "it is the wrong time," or experiencing feelings of not being understood or not good enough. What you resist persists, which means that the same situations will keep presenting themselves until you decide to change. Scarlett O'Hara's reaction to Rhett Butler leaving her in *Gone with the Wind* was, "I'll think about that tomorrow"—a classic line of resistance to change. The emotion that fuels resistance is fear.

Having a clear vision of what you want can often avert the fear of change. Change means a fresh perspective. Invite in the new by having a replacement plan to fill the gap once you release the old. The gap is one of the most frightening aspects of change, so having a plan will help you to feel more at ease and allow you to move effortlessly toward your objective.

Love to Fear, Fearing Love

In her book *A Course in Miracles*, Helen Schucman states that there are only two basic human emotions: love and fear. If your actions are not based on love, then on some level they must be rooted in fear. Fear resides where there is no love, and love is an inside job. For that reason, if we loved ourselves there would be no place left for fear to hide.

Love is an important aspect of everyone's life. The way to combat fear is to fill your life with love. Love attracts love as like attracts like. Susan Jeffers, the author of *Feel the Fear and Do it Anyway*, writes, "When we give from a place of love ... more usually comes back to us than we could ever have imagined." This is not a trick—it is that simple; the tricky part is loving yourself.

Reports from those who have lived through near-death experiences all include the same theme about love—we are here on earth to learn to love. Many who have lived through this event have retained information from a place between life and death that they say is full of light. Both adults and children who have been to this place consistently return with the same message. We need to learn to live consciously with love in our hearts—to make our every decision based on love—to replace anger, fear, and hatred with love, and to remember that by forgiving others we forgive ourselves. Philosopher Ralph Waldo Trine said, "Love is everything. It is the key to life, and its influences are those that move the world."

If you were to die right now, and you were obliged to give an account of your life, could you honestly say that you had given love unconditionally or based all of your decisions on love? By loving others unconditionally, you in turn will receive love; this is a basic law of attraction. A life worth recalling is one full of love. This opinion was expressed by Canadian poet Henry Drummond when he said, "You will find as you look back upon your life that the moments that stand out, the moments when you have really lived, are the moments when you have done things in the spirit of love." Your unconditional love will attract an abundance of blessings into your life. But do not take my word for it; try it for yourself.

Beth was a client who came to one of my workshops on healing after her divorce. As with many women, Beth had issues around attracting a mate. She felt unloved, unwanted, and rejected, and had very low self-esteem. When she came to the workshop, she had no idea what to expect or why she was there. Over the course of a few days, she learned that her self-image was key to the energy she attracted in her life. Although many people are aware of the concept that like attracts like, Beth was unaware that loving yourself can invite love into your life.

She applied some of the tools she learned in the class, such as changing negative words into positive, focusing on what she wanted rather than what she did not want, and meditating on the truth of who she was, unlike her poor self-image of who she thought she was. The new friends she made during the class supported her on this journey. A few months later she came to see me for a private consultation. She had made a complete turnaround in her life to the extent that she was now teaching others about the laws of attraction. Although she was not in a permanent relationship, she was dating and felt good about herself. What she had not realized initially was that her wish was to return to herself. She just knew that something had to change, and it did!

WISH PRACTICE:
Getting What You Want

☆ ★ ★ ☆ ⋅ ✩ ⋅ ☆ ★ ★ ★ ☆ ⋅ ✩ ⋅ ☆ ⋅ ★ ★ ☆ ⋅ ✩ ⋅ ☆

Find a comfortable position, close your eyes, take some deep breaths, and relax. The more relaxed you are, the easier it will be to focus. Calm your mind, and turn your attention to your breathing ... release any tension by breathing into it ... focus your mind on relaxing each area of your body until you feel completely comfortable and at ease.

When you are ready, begin to visualize yourself with every-thing that you want in your life: the perfect home, perfect job, perfect relationship. Create a whole picture in your mind, including all the details: the weather, where you are, whom you are with, and what time of day, month, and year it is. Make this as real as you can. How does this picture make you feel? What thoughts come up for you? Do you feel joy or fear? Do you believe you are ready to receive the gift of abundance in your life? Are there any areas of tension in your body that are related to this feeling? Take some time to explore your feelings.

When you are ready, commence the return to waking con-sciousness. As you do so, visualize a waterfall of light above your head, washing that image away, and cleansing every area of your being. Take some deep breaths and open your eyes.

Record your revelations, feelings, and fears in your wish journal. Spend some time reading through your text. If there are any negative statements, write the opposite positive statement next to them. Positive statements are truths; nega-tive statements are challenges. Accept this wisdom by saying it over and over again, like a chant or an affirmation. Write all your truths on separate pieces of paper and put them any-where you will regularly come across them—on the fridge, in the bathroom, at work on your desk, anywhere and every-where they will be observed. Alternatively, you can use all the positive words and statements to create one or more affirmations. Again, place them in areas where they will be visible on a daily basis.

☆ ⋆ ★ ⋆ ☆ ⋆ ☆ ⋆ ☆ ⋆ ★ ⋆ ☆ ⋆ ☆ ⋆ ☆ ⋆ ★ ⋆ ☆ ⋆ ☆ ⋆ ☆

WISH SENSE TIPS

1. Fear is your greatest enemy. "Feel the fear and do it anyway!" Say yes to the opportunities life has to offer; otherwise, you cannot enjoy life to the fullest.

2. Do you fear success or do you fear failure? Identify what you really want in your life, and when you get it, do not be afraid to greet it with open arms.

3. What you resist persists! Recognize that the same old situations will continue to present themselves until you make the decision to change.

4. There are only two emotions: love and fear. If your actions are not based on love, then they must be rooted in fear to some degree.

5. Keep your words sweet in case you have to eat them! Language, language, language. Words have energy, so choose them carefully.

Feelings of fear can prevent you from moving forward and enjoying your life. I recently met a woman who had suffered a heart attack during a stressful period in her life. At her job, she was encouraged by her company to work as much as eighty hours a week. Eventually the strain created a health wake-up call, and yet eighteen months later she was contemplating reemployment with the same company. Her passion was writing, although she would not consider a literary career as her next step. Instead, she chose to stay with something that was familiar, thereby ensuring an income while avoiding her success and failure gremlins.

Change means letting go of old habits. This can be challenging. Habits are like a pair of old slippers; they are comfortable and they can define who we are and what we believe about ourselves. Serious illness is often a call to take stock of one's life, and this usually involves major change. Change rarely occurs when you focus on loss, such as loss of income. Instead, think of what you can gain from a situation. Learning to act in a new way and envisioning the person you want to be will be akin to meeting a new friend. You may be suspicious at first, even downright stubborn, but once the new behavior is incorporated into your being, you will reap the benefits and notice improvements in every area of your life.

5

The Natural Spell for Your Wishes to Grow

**Not getting what you want is sometimes
a wonderful stroke of luck.**

—The Dalai Lama

Y ou do not always get what you want in the way you expect. Sometimes your needs and desires are both in alignment and will be one and the same—a cause for celebration. However, occasionally you are just not meant to get the particular thing you yearn for.

This was demonstrated to me some years ago. Shortly after I qualified as a nurse, I applied for my first staffing position on a surgical ward where I had worked as part of my training. The week before the interview, I had a heated conversation with the senior nurse in charge of that section about the state of nursing. I made the mistake of disagreeing with her on one or two points, which was not well received. To my dismay, the same senior nurse interviewed me the following week, and needless to say I was not offered the job. Instead, I immediately started work in the intensive care unit where I had planned to go later in the year.

After working there for six months, I went through one of the most difficult periods of my life, but fate had been kind and allowed me to work in an area where staffing levels were high, which consequently meant that I could take as much personal time as I needed. In addition, I was offered the love and support of my colleagues, some of whom I still count among my friends. At the time of my first job interview, I did not appreciate how fortunate I was to be rejected for the position. But I soon began to realize that I could not have

71

planned my life more perfectly. Although I had wanted the surgical job, it would not have provided me with the time and support I would later require. Instead, I was given the job that offered me exactly what I needed for that particular period of my life.

Reasons to Be Cheerful

One of my treasured books as a child was about a young boy who had the gift of clairvoyance, commonly known as second sight. The book, called *The Boy Who Saw True*, is a combination of diaries the author kept as a child and letters he wrote as an adult to his wife while traveling. The author's name is still unknown. It is alleged that his relatives would have been embarrassed by their ignorance of his gifts, although it was eventually published after his immediate family passed away.

The author had been brought up in a well-to-do household during the Victorian era in the north of England. As a child he did not realize that others could not see the things he clearly saw. He was able to communicate with the departed souls of his relatives, in particular his grandfather, who was one of his most regular visitors.

One day, the boy fell ill and took to his bed. It transpired that he suffered from a "weak heart," which meant that he could no longer attend school and would have to be tutored at home. His deceased grandfather communicated to him that he would be glad of the heart problem in the future. Meanwhile, the spirits had arranged for him to be tutored by a gentleman who would understand, support, and nurture his gifts. This duly happened, much to his satisfaction. Some years later, when the First World War broke out, the boy—who was now a man—was unable to join the forces to fight for his country due to his weak heart. While this condition was unwelcome when he was a child, as an adult he indeed realized why his grandfather had said he would one day be grateful for the diagnosis. It was, in fact, a fortunate predicament since few men survived the Great War.

We are not always aware of the greater picture. Knowing that you are living in perfect alignment with a universal plan requires faith, especially when you do not get what you want. Everything is as it should be. Understanding this allows you to relax and live your life in harmony.

It Is Natural

Nature has a way of showing us the process of life. For example, flower seeds are sown during springtime. They lay down roots and strengthen their bodies, preparing for transformation. Shoots sprout up from the ground, twisting and twining, growing in the glory of the sunlight. Their final achievement, an expression of their love, is a flower. Plants go through a natural growth period before they allow their flowers to blossom. Flowering takes a lot of energy. If they blossomed too soon, it could jeopardize the life of the whole plant. The contemporary poet David Whyte expressed our potential to blossom as a choice only we humans have. He said, "Man is the only species privileged to refuse its own flowering."

We all need time to blossom, and yet we are impatient and expect to skip the growth period and move right into flowering. The universe is kind when it does not grant some of our wishes; it knows there is another growth opportunity awaiting our attention. It will only send you what you are capable of handling, nothing more and nothing less. But when you have grown and are in full bloom, you will be mature enough to be able to handle whatever the universe has to offer. You will have strong roots based on your experiences and an upright stem, showing that you are capable of handling responsibility. Your leaves will be the embodiment of your ability to nourish and heal yourself. And, when you are ready and at the peak of your development, you will blossom. Your flower will be an expression of the love and appreciation you have for yourself. And you will be ready and open to receive your heart's desire.

Empty of Expectations; Full of Expectancy

One of the secrets to manifesting your wishes is expecting without expectation. Have you noticed that when you expect something to happen it generally does, and yet when you have expectations, it either takes longer to manifest or does not happen at all? It is healthy to expect your wish to be granted, and yet it is doomed to failure as soon as you set up an expectation. There is a difference.

Expecting assumes action, such as expecting to pay for an item in a shop, or expecting the sun to rise in the morning. Hence, we let go of the things we expect because we are confident they will manifest. Expectation, on the other hand, is the act of hoping, which implies anticipation rather than action. An expectation is more possessive; it is an idea that is held on to and creates much disappointment when it does not materialize. It is similar to waiting for the phone to ring after a job interview. You expect to get a job, but your expectation is to get this job.

When you have an expectation and it fails to manifest, what is your first reaction? Do you say, "I knew it wouldn't happen!"? This thought may appear to be a spontaneous reaction, but more than likely it originated deep within your subconscious and is part of the reason the job didn't manifest. It is likely that somewhere in the back of your mind lurks a thought that is limiting your experience. One way to remedy this is by making a conscious effort to let go of your expectations.

For example, if you are looking for a new relationship, expect to be in a relationship, but do not have any expectations about how the relationship will develop. Letting go of your expectations enables you to release the image you have formed of how love usually manifests for you, and allows the relationship to grow in its own way. Similarly, when you make a wish, expect that it will be granted, but do not have any expectations about how, when, and where it will manifest. Let it go. This allows the wish to manifest in its own time, and sometimes in the most unexpected way.

Believing Is Seeing!

Occasionally your wish manifests straight in front of your face, and yet you are unable to recognize it. Our experiences shape who we are and play a major part in what we expect in our lives. The same holds true with wishing. Over the years I have learned that wishes really can come true, and sometimes the trick is recognizing when a wish has been granted. This often comes with experience.

A friend of mine, Wendy, decided that she wanted to date a man of substance, someone who could support both her and her family, as well as give her the love that she craved. The saying "you can't see the forest for the trees" aptly described her inability to recognize the manifestation of her individual creative power.

She made her wish and then sat back to wait for the man of her dreams. However, she was totally oblivious to the multitude of men lined up on her doorstep. She was looking for Superman, and none of them fit the bill. As a result, she thought her wish had not been granted, even though she was entertaining a constant flow of men. Once she realized her mistake, she recognized just how powerful she was to create so many men willing to take on the job. Recognizing when a wish has manifested often requires a change of focus, or a friend who can see your life better than you can.

Whatever You Are Ready for Is Ready for You!

The saying "when the flower blooms, the bees come uninvited" means that when you are ready for opportunities, they will come naturally. Although my wishes are frequently fulfilled, I am always surprised by the apparent simplicity of their manifestation. I trust that I will receive the outcome of my wish in one form or another. If you make a wish and it does not materialize, do not immediately believe that it is your fault, or that you do not deserve it. Trust that you will receive the answer to your wish, although it may not come in the form you originally expected. Remain open to the possibilities and, as author Marianne Williamson put it, don't ask for more flowers, just a bigger vase. In other words, you are a vessel for the abundance of the universe. So instead of asking for more abundance, be a bigger vessel and be ready to accept with open arms the abundance available to you.

Understanding the Reasons Behind Life Events

I wonder how my life would have changed had some of my wishes come true—or manifested at the time I asked for them. Think about a time when you did not get what you asked for, or at least it appeared that way. What would have changed in your life if you had received what you wanted? Would you be where you are today? Consider what you might have missed from your current life had you taken a different path. It is important to recognize and appreciate the reasons why your life moves in certain directions. This insight may help you to be grateful for the gift of your life as it is right now and aid in your perception of the greater picture. We do not always get to see the big picture, but we can acknowledge that there is one.

For instance, during World War II my father joined the Royal Air Force. To determine their individual assignments, new pilots were allocated tests. For the first test, he was led into a darkened room and positioned in a chair facing a console similar to a computer screen. Once the door was closed, leaving the room in complete darkness, it was his signal to record everything he saw on the screen. At the end of the test, my father was given a 100 percent night vision rating, which meant that he would be assigned night flights—a safer option than flying during daylight hours. But his night vision rating had a helping hand. At the beginning of the test he had heard a loud clicking noise behind him. It turned out that this sound stemmed from a clip coming loose from the back of his shirt, originally placed there to prevent him from leaning forward. Without his knowledge the undone clip had allowed him to lean forward and easily view the console screen, awarding him the perfect score.

For the next test, he had to fly a plane with an instructor. My father was a meticulous person and an excellent pilot, yet on this particular flight he made what he considered to be a serious error on landing the plane. This error was the second contribution toward saving his life. It meant that he would be stationed in the Orient rather than assigned to take part in campaigns over Europe, where the vast majority of pilots lost their lives.

There is one more piece to this story. One day when he was in Ceylon, now called Sri Lanka, he caught sight of a woman he knew riding along in a rickshaw. He had met her some years before at a dance on the pier in the local town where he grew up. She was in Ceylon with the Royal Navy, working on Lord Louis Mountbatten's staff. Their friendship was rekindled and a few years later he married her—my mother. Had he not been stationed in the Orient maybe he would not have met up with my mother, I would not have been born, and you would not be reading this book!

Many things in our lives happen for a reason. My father's story is no different from any other. Even his supposed mistakes appear to be a part of a bigger picture. We are not always privy to the panoramic view of our lives, yet there is much going on behind the scenes that guides us in the most rewarding direction. These rewards may not be what we would consider fruitful. Some are seemingly absent of all joy. Just keep in mind the bigger picture, and this will help you to accept the gifts and challenges that life has to offer you; it may be that one of these gifts or challenges will help you to achieve your wish.

Wish In-Sight

The main ingredients to prepare yourself for the activity of wish sense have been provided, but before you start wishing for the world to fall into your lap, first consider the importance of energy exchange. Be conscious that for every action there is an equal and opposite reaction. We have all heard the Biblical expression "as you sow, so shall you reap."

This universal law of cause and effect is known in Buddhism and Hinduism as karma. Similar to the eye-for-an-eye saga found in the Bible, karma is an ancient system that sought to explain why good things happen to bad people and bad things happen to good people, a system for liberation that is generally associated with previous lifetimes. The principal concept is that gifts or pain experienced during one's present life are attributed to past, present, and future good or bad deeds from this or other existences through time. Karmic debts or rewards are accumulated and experienced in the current lifetime, amassed from previous lifetimes, and potentially accrued from future lifetimes as well. Karma can be so immense and life-changing that it is often called lightning karma due to the swiftness of its action.

The manifestation of your wish could depend upon the kind of karma you have amassed during this lifetime. Karmic points are awarded for good deeds involving sincere acts of compassion, love, generosity, and gratitude without thought of reward or acknowledgment. Acts of kindness come in all shapes and sizes. It really does not matter how or what you do; the thought behind the action is what counts. If you are being nice to someone because you think you will get more points and into the karmic good books, then think again. Any notion of karmic reward will negate the kindness because your only sentiment is for yourself and not for another.

Karma is similar to the law of attraction because karmic energy is drawn toward you in response to your thoughts and actions; it is not awarded by one particular person or being. The main focus of this law is that like attracts like. So when you offer kindness to another, you will invite a reciprocal kindness to you. The same applies if you do something that is less than kind—you can attract an equal disservice to yourself. You naturally generate karma by your deeds and by your desire for certain experiences. However, not all karma is quite so straightforward. Some karmic gifts or penance come from deeds that have been performed in existences other than your current one. Life works with this magnetic law and pulls to you that which will serve you for your highest good.

So, good deeds create positive karma and, in the practice of wish sense, we want to call on and generate as much good karma as we can. Now, consider the karma you are creating with your specific wish. If you wish for something negative, remember that the energy will be returned to you in one form or another.

This is not to say that you will not receive your wish, but that it comes at a price. If, on the other hand, you wish for something positive, not only do you need the right consciousness to receive it, but you also require a good karma bank account to draw from for its manifestation. It is like money, only this is the exchange of energy. When you create something, energy is spent and has to be replaced. Normally this energy is substituted by your own good karma. Occasionally, you will have nothing left in your account, but the universe is kind and allows you an overdraft facility, similar to buying on credit. It does not necessarily mean you will get exactly what you want, but it may help you to make the first step toward achieving the manifestation of your wish.

Lightning karma manifests immediately to replace spent energy without the use of wish sense. I was recently reminded of this truth. London is full of street musicians and beggars. One day on my way to work, I gave away all the money I had with me to the people on the streets—not much really, about ten dollars, but I was left without any cash in my purse. It was a warm day and I was thirsty, so I rifled through my bag in search of change for the soft drink machine. I managed to scrape together the exact amount needed. I put the money into the slot, pushed the appropriate buttons, and to my surprise the machine not only gave me my drink, but change as well, adding up to ten dollars. Giving is receiving. I had no thought of a return on my money given away and yet my reward was instant.

Avoid making a greedy or selfish wish. Probably neither will be realized, but the energy of your desire could have negative consequences. Since you get what you give out, use your integrity and take responsibility for both your thoughts and your wishes, lest your wish come true.

For instance, if you lust after another's lover, think of the repercussions of your selfish desire. In other words, it does not matter if your wish comes true or not; it is the thought that counts! Just be aware of the backlash you could set in motion. Remember, everything is energy. Instead of wishing for a particular person to be in your life, it is preferable to wish for the energy or the essence of that person. This way you are more likely to receive what you want without challenging karma. In essence, you are the creator. You hold the truth of manifestation within you, so use it wisely.

WISH PRACTICE:
Discover How Open You Are to Receiving

★ ★ ★ ★ ☆ ★ ☆ ★ ☆ ★ ★ ★ ★ ☆ ★ ☆ ★ ☆ ★ ★ ★ ★ ☆ ★ ☆ ★ ☆

Sometimes we ask for things and then say we are not ready for them. Are you prepared to accept the wonderful gifts that the universe has in store for you? This exercise, based on one from Louise Hay's wonderful book *You Can Heal Your Life*, will help you to discover just how open you are to receiving the abundance available to you.

Find a comfortable position, close your eyes, and relax. Focus your attention on your breathing. Allow each breath to move through your body, and release any tension by breathing into it. Do this until you feel completely comfortable and relaxed.

When you are ready, imagine you are standing in front of an ocean, with just the expanse of the sea ahead of you. Behind you is a large, empty container. Your task is to fill the container with water from the ocean using whatever utensils are available to you in your imagination. Look around and find something that will help you to perform this task. When you have filled the container to your satisfaction, take some deep breaths and return to waking consciousness.

★ ★ ★ ★ ☆ ★ ☆ ★ ☆ ★ ★ ★ ★ ☆ ★ ☆ ★ ☆ ★ ★ ★ ★ ☆ ★ ☆ ★ ☆

Water is the universal symbol of abundance, prosperity, and love, so your ability to fill the container represents your capacity to receive love and abundance. If you employed small utensils such as a spoon, cup, or bucket, you perhaps have a cautious attitude and may not be able to receive the abundance or/and love you deserve. If you took the container to the ocean or used a pipeline to fill it, or even imagined that it was full without any effort on your part, then you are almost certainly willing to accept the wonder of love and abundance on offer.

While doing this meditation, one of my students told me that she started out with a spoon, but created a pipeline from the ocean to the container. Another person just thought the container full and it was. You can repeat this exercise and change the way you approach the task. Recognize what feelings come up for you as you do this and record them in your wish journal.

WISH SENSE TIPS

1. Not getting what you want is sometimes a wonderful stroke of luck. Accept that the universe will give you exactly what you need right now.
2. Everything happens for a reason. We are not always aware of the greater picture.
3. Blossoming is a process, so be patient. If you try to open a bud when it is not ready, the flower does not contain all that it needs to fully express its beauty.
4. Empty of expectations; full of expectancy. Expect your wish to be granted, but do not have any expectations about how it will manifest.
5. Whatever you are ready for is ready for you! If you are not ready for it, then it will not come to you. If you are ready, even if you do not know it, it will find you.

Impatience is defined as wanting things your way. Imagine for a moment that you were born and then suddenly transported from the moment of birth to the point you are at now without all the experiences in between. You are able to walk and talk and function in the world, but you are unaware of the opportunities the world has to offer because you lack experience. This is similar to a flower blossoming before it is ready. When you have patience, you can get on with your life and cherish the joy of each moment. If you are waiting for something to happen, and you want it right now, then you will miss the beauty of your life and will be unable to appreciate all your blessings.

Part III
Wish Sense

A recipe for miracles: one dose of intention,
a pinch of focus, and a whole lot of faith.

—Unknown

6

The Seven Principles to Creating Your Perfect Wish

If you can dream it, you can do it.
—Walt Disney

There are seven principles involved in wish sense, a number that is associated with luck, magic, and mysticism. The number seven was thought to have immense power because it is formed as a result of the alchemical combination of the female three with the masculine four. Seventh heaven may be so termed due to this fusion and balance of the male and female principles. The seventh child is supposed to possess special gifts. There are seven colors in a rainbow, seven rays on the head of the Statue of Liberty relating to the seven continents, seven notes in a major scale, seven chakras or energy wheels within the body, Seven Wonders of the World, and according to the Bible, it took seven days to create the Earth.

Seven Principles of Wish Sense

1. Intention. This is your wish, the destination that guides the pathway of energy and action.
2. Focus. Visualize your wish in its entirety.
3. Want it with all of your heart. Affirm the essence of your wish in your life.
4. Ask once. Believe it to conceive it!
5. Have an attitude of gratitude. Say thank you both before and after your wish has manifested.

6. Wish-tell. Do you need to share your wish? Use your intuition to guide you to the truth and the right person.

7. Let it go. It is now a matter for the universe.

Now is the ideal moment to take the wish card out of its envelope and reflect on your original wish. Do not change your wish yet. Whether you decide to alter it or make a new one, the following principles contain all the information you require to construct your wish in the correct form as well as the precise technique to manifest it. These principles contain knowledge that you have already learned, in addition to new material that will support you in creating the right wish for you. Follow these steps one by one, and use them as a guideline to your own creative power. Allow yourself some leeway; whatever works for you is the right way, provided it stays within the confines of universal law. Remember to complete the exercises at the end of each section before moving on to the next.

The First Principle: Wish Intention

Now that you recognize your wonderful ability to create anything you desire in your life, you have the responsibility to decide what you really want before creating it. This is an important aspect of wish fulfillment. Think about it carefully. Are you asking for something because it is what you want, or because it will get you what you want?

Most people make the mistake of wishing to win the lottery because they believe it will change some aspect of their lives for the better. And why do they not win? Because it was not their deepest wish—it was not really what they wanted. They asked for something to get them what they wanted, in this case money! With respect to wish sense, this attitude is limiting because it is conditional and entirely dependent upon a specific way something will materialize, which is akin to putting all of your eggs in one basket. Consequently, nine times out of ten, these wishes do not come to fruition.

The most important principle of wish sense is intention: knowing what you want. For example, if you wish for a new home, is it the home you want or the security it represents? Maybe it is the sense of independence that owning a home creates, or the new neighbors who go with it, or the area you want to be in. Or is your home so dilapidated that you hate the very sight of it and think that a new home would make you feel happier? What is it you really want—money, security, or your own space?

You learned earlier how to discover your initial motivation. Now you are trying to access how you would feel if this were a part of your life. Take a moment to think about this. Is there a reason behind your need for something to be a part of your life? What would change in your life as a result of your wish being granted? Capture that feeling, and look at the change, because therein lies the answer. The outcome or the essence of the outcome is what you should be asking for.

If you are in need of a rest and wish for a vacation in the Caribbean, the outcome would be more than just a wonderful sun-tan. It would allow you time to relax, put your feet up, read a good book, eat exotic food, and enjoy the romance of a tropical paradise. Now, essentially this is what you should be asking for, and I will tell you why. If you wish for the vacation, granted, it will likely get you what you want, but if you cannot afford the time or the money to go, what then? Does this mean that your wish will not come true?

Not necessarily, but it could take longer because not only was the wish limited, but your perception of how the wish could materialize may also influence its manifestation. If the wish had been for time to relax on a beach enjoying the heat of the sun (the outcome), then one way or another you would be sipping cocktails to the sound of lapping waves from a warm, tropical sea. In other words, asking for what you want and not for something to get you what you want will increase the probability of receiving your wish.

There is another level to this. There is a fine line between being specific and being too general. The above wish example would get you what you want, but it may not come in the way that you desire. It could manifest through positive channels or as the result of nega-tive circumstances. For instance, the Caribbean vacation may come as the result of a relative who is dying there, or a friend who is stuck there because of a burglary and needs your help, or due to you having an illness that can only be cured by being in this particular place. So when you make your wish, specify that it will manifest through positive circumstances, and remember to make positive statements and not negative ones as part of your wish. Try not to specify how your wish will manifest; just spell out that you wish this to be for your highest good and the outcome of positive events in your life.

As another example, let's say you want to join an exclusive health club but cannot afford the membership fees. What effect would a year's membership have on your life? You could get into shape, use all the facilities available to pamper yourself, and feel a sense of achievement. If you ask for membership, you limit your wish, because you are asking for something to get you something you want—better shape, pampering, and achievement. But by wishing for the outcome, one way or another, you will either be walking through those health club doors on a regular basis, or achieving the outcome of your wish in another way, and maybe in a different place. Remember that the intention behind this wish is to manifest it for positive reasons and not because something negative happened.

How would it feel to have your wish come true? If you are wishing for a promotion, wish for the outcome of the promotion and everything that goes with it. How does it feel when you imagine yourself experiencing that new position? Capture the feeling and wish for that feeling. If you want a new home, relationship, or career, imagine yourself in that situation and how it makes you feel. Do you feel a sense of security, power, comfort, and love? This is what you should be asking for: the outcome.

Your intention should always be for the highest good and not to cause harm. Remember the karmic system of energy exchange and its implications. Wishing harm on someone will create an energy that will eventually be returned to you. Be realistic about your intentions when making your wish.

Completing the following sentences and recording them in your journal will help you to recognize the intention behind your wish and the difference it will make in your life:

I want to make this wish because...
The difference it will make in my life will be...
It is not in my life right now because...

Consider what you have written, and assess whether your wish needs to be changed. For example, you may wish for a promotion because you want an increase in salary, more challenges, higher status, and more respect. You could also then take extra holidays, build the home addition you always wanted, be enthusiastic about using your knowledge, and gain the respect of colleagues as a result. So why haven't you been promoted yet? Perhaps the opportunity was not there, you were not in the right place at the right time, you are not the boss's favorite, and you have not applied for the job. So a promotion for you really means that you will be using your talents to their full capacity, gaining acknowledgment from your colleagues, and creating an abundance of both time and money to do the things that you have always wanted to do.

Now put this into a feeling. How would it feel to use your talent—exciting, exhilarating, satisfying? How would it feel to have the extra money—free, secure, safe, abundant? Just be aware of how something manifesting in your life will make you feel. The feeling or essence of what you want is the key to manifesting your wish. So, your intention may be for a job that is more satisfying, exciting, and abundant rather than a promotion that may not present itself in your current situation.

WISH PRACTICE:
Wishing Dreams

☆ ★ ★ ☆ ★ ☆ ★ ☆ ★ ★ ☆ ★ ☆ ★ ☆ ★ ★ ☆ ★ ☆ ★ ☆

Make a list of everything you want in your life. Include absolutely everything from the Rolls-Royce to the outdoor Jacuzzi, from a date with your favorite movie star to a trip around the world. Do not skimp on this—really go for it! Be outrageous! What do you want? When you have finished, read through the list and one by one write next to each potential wish how it would change your life. Limit yourself to one-word answers. Try to include all your feelings in this one word and take note of any repeated words. Now read the list again. Is there a theme? Are you repeatedly asking for the same thing or the same feeling? If there are repeated words, consider including these in a wish. Highlight them in your wish journal to be used at a later date.

☆ ★ ★ ★ ☆ · ☆ · ☆ ★ ☆ ★ ☆ · ☆ · ☆ · ★ ★ ☆ · ☆ · ☆

Fran is a gifted artist and client. She tended to keep her beautiful creations to herself. Friends and relatives encouraged her to promote her work, yet the first time she did this neither she nor her fan club got the desired response. Again, she retreated from displaying or selling her art. The Wishing Dreams exercise helped her to understand that her intention was mixed up with her fear. She wanted to bring joy into people's lives, but she feared rejection at the same time. Once she realized this, she shifted her energy and began looking at her pictures as little pieces of love and visualizing that people would receive the gift of love just by being in their presence. This took the pressure off her and helped her to once more exhibit her work. The response was a blessing. She saw her work as a gift of gratitude and love that was taken into the homes of those who visited her gallery.

WISH SENSE TIPS

1. Ask for what you want. If you want new clothes, do not ask for the money to buy them; ask for the clothes and the feeling that a new wardrobe would give you.
2. Are you excited? Your wish should invoke excitement and enthusiasm. You should get a wonderful feeling of elation at the prospect of receiving your wish. If you do not, then you are probably asking for the wrong thing.

3. Be realistic. Have a clear vision of what you want based in reality. If you are a two-hundred-pound, five-foot brunette, do not wish to be a one-hundred-twenty-pound, six-foot blonde by next Monday. Your wish would more authentically be along the lines of loving yourself and feeling good about yourself. Imagine how that feels. Does it feel good? If it does not, then something else is at work. Get to the feeling you wish to have in your life, and one way or another that feeling will be honored.

4. Decide what you really want. Be conscious that you are making your true wish.

5. What would change if you had what you wanted? Capture that feeling. Look to the change/outcome—this is what you should be asking for.

6. Your intention is always for the highest good. Remember, your wish holds power, and wishing harm to others will be returned to you manyfold.

7. Count your blessings. Learn to appreciate the wonderful gifts that are already present in your life.

There is no point in asking for something to get you what you want, especially when you already have it. Most people assume that what will make them happy is something completely different from what they have right now. Often this is a new relationship, new job, new home, and so on. Maybe it is simpler than that. It could be that what is needed is a new perspective on something that is already present. Ask for the outcome; it works more often than not!

The Second Principle: Wish Hocus-Focus

A few years ago I wrote my Ideal Man list, an inventory of all the qualities I admired and wanted at that time in the man of my dreams. The usual qualities of tall, dark, and handsome came into it, along with some very specific qualities. Three weeks later I met the man who matched my description, right down to the very last quality.

Unfortunately, he was married. I completely forgot to say "available," so that was the end of that relationship!

The point of this story is to be specific. If you are making a wish for a relationship, for example, make sure that you specify available, in your age group, and preferably on this planet. The more specific you are, the more likely you will attract exactly what you want. Of course there is being specific and then there is being too detailed. For instance, if you order a pizza, you ask for everything you want on that pizza, including the kind of crust you want. What you do not say is that you want the crust made from flour. At the back of your mind this part of your request is obvious and it is a no-brainer. That goes for your wishes too. Certain aspects of your wishes do not need to be expressed.

There is a saying, "name it to claim it!" This does not mean that by naming someone, they are yours. Wishing does not work that way. You cannot wish for the movie star of your dreams to be a part of your life any more than you can wish to be taller. But you can wish for the feeling that person would give you if he or she were a part of your life. You can wish for the essence. So naming something to claim it means to name that sense or feeling. This leads into being specific about what you want.

For instance, let's say you are hungry and go into a sandwich shop. You are offered a salami sandwich as soon as you walk in. Although you are having a little trouble deciding what you want, you do know that you do not want a salami sandwich. Instead you ask for a cheese sandwich, but when it comes it is still not right. Oh yes, you wanted brown bread, not white. So it is sent back and another sandwich is presented to you, this time cheese on brown bread. But you realize that it just would not be right without some tomato. And so, the sandwich is returned and replaced by a cheese and tomato on brown bread. But where is the mayonnaise? And so it goes until you specify what you want, which is actually the wonderful feeling of being satisfied by a sandwich that is made to your specifications, without actually asking for that particular sandwich. Get it? You will! Imagine, just for a moment, how it feels to bite into your favorite sandwich. That's it, imagine how luscious it is, how mouth-wateringly satisfying it is. Isn't it just the most delicious thing you have ever tasted? Now capture that feeling and you are halfway to manifesting it.

There are two sides to this. It is all very well being specific, but the more specific you are, the longer it takes to get exactly what you want; so if you have a long list, do not expect it to arrive by tomorrow. It is similar to asking a real estate agent to look for a new house. If you specify that you want it on the beach with six bedrooms, wooden floors, bay windows, a garage, a six-acre garden including a waterfall, and woods at the back with your nearest neighbor at least a mile away, it is going to take a little more time than simply asking for a two-bedroom apartment.

Do not get me wrong: being specific works. I asked for an apartment with wooden floors, big windows, and a chaise longue, and I got it three months later. I needed a place that would make me feel safe and secure, was inexpensive, and would reflect my bohemian side. The apartment belonged to a psychic artist friend who was leaving the country. She did not want to let the apartment go; she just wanted someone to sublet it from her just in case she decided to return. It was in a women's cooperative in one of the most bohemian and expensive areas of London, and it was perfect for me at that time.

Had I added flowery wallpaper to my list, it probably would have taken a little longer. Be specific, but keep it as simple as you can. Just be aware that if you have a five-page list, it is going to take longer. By the time it manifests, you may well be drawing your pension, and it might not be the most important thing on your wish list anymore.

A camera requires focusing in order to take a clear picture, or else the resulting photograph will be blurred. Similarly, focusing on your wish will achieve a clear outcome. Otherwise, the payoff may not be exactly what you want. Once you decide on a wish, make it the center of your attention. Remember: where attention goes, energy flows. Picture what you want. Make your imagination work for you. Put all of your senses into creating an image of receiving your wish. This way, nothing is excluded as you create a whole picture of your heart's desire. Your subconscious mind will realize your wish by reproducing the image, provided the image remains the same.

WISH PRACTICE:
Visualizing Your Wish

☆ ★ ★ ★ ☆ ★ ☆ ★ ☆ ★ ★ ★ ☆ ★ ☆ ★ ☆ ★ ★ ★ ☆ ★ ☆ ★ ☆

Remember that the subconscious mind works in pictures. In chapter 4 you learned that visualization is key to manifesting your wishes. So just for a moment, close your eyes and begin to visualize your wish as if it is already a part of your life. See it in its entirety; get a sense of the feeling that goes with your wish. Stay with your visualization until it actually feels like it is a part of your life.

Once you have done this, let the picture go, but remember the feeling; this is the key to manifesting your wish. If you could capture the feeling in one word, what would it be? Write this word in your wish journal and highlight or underline it for future reference. When you become an expert, you will be able to visualize and feel your wish in an instant.

☆ ★ ★ ★ ☆ ★ ☆ ★ ☆ ★ ★ ★ ☆ ★ ☆ ★ ☆ ★ ★ ★ ☆ ★ ☆ ★ ☆

My friend Tom owns a real estate agency with interests worldwide. Despite all of his savvy marketing strategies, his business was suffering. In his college days he had been an athlete and he knew the power of visualization, so using this tool to save his business wasn't such a stretch for him. Every morning he visualized new clients coming into his office. He saw them congratulating him on his success, handing over checks, shaking hands on a deal, and going away happy. By simply visualizing new clients coming into his life, he put his business back on track and almost doubled his client base over the course of six months.

WISH SENSE TIPS

1. Be specific. Make your wish as specific as you can. There is no point asking for something and then being disappointed because it is not exactly what you wanted.

2. Keep it simple. The more complicated your wish, the longer it will take. This is not cast in stone of course, but if you liken it to a recipe with lots of ingredients, then it might take you longer to create the dish.

3. Make it short and sweet. The lengthier it is, the less likely your wish will manifest immediately. This is not to say that it will not manifest; it may just take a little more time.

4. Name it to claim it! Name the essence of your wish; capture the feeling. If there is something or someone you want, and it or the person appears to be out of your reach, think about what is at the heart of your desire. Use one word that epitomizes your wish. This essence is what you should be asking for.

5. Some wishes are achieved in steps. If you want a promotion, write out the steps required to achieve your objective. You may need to wish for a step at a time rather than the whole objective.

6. Picture your wish in its entirety. Visualization is one of the most powerful, environmentally friendly tools at your disposal.

Clarity of both heart and mind is what the Buddhists call Diamond Consciousness. The first step to obtaining clarity is to cast away your fears and preconceptions and be honest with yourself. If you could have anything or be anybody, and nothing stood in your way, what would you wish for? If you want to be a great football player or a world-famous artist, what is it about these roles that would make you happy? In order for your wish to manifest, you need to focus on the right thing. Once you have recognized what this is, you can take the necessary steps toward the attainment of your wish.

The Third Principle: Wish Hearts

When you were a child, what technique did you use to get exactly what you wanted? Were you the type to have temper tantrums? Did you say, "I want, I want, I want," and it would be given to you? Or did you whimper and then put on a warm and syrupy look, with a few sweet nothings thrown in for good measure? Would that get you what you wanted? If it worked then and still works now, then good luck to you. But there will come a time when you need to take responsibility for your life.

Think back and try to remember an instance when you wished for something to be a part of your life, something you wanted with all of your heart. Against the odds it miraculously appeared, not through tantrums or duress, but due to something completely different. Do you remember the circumstances that led to this manifestation of your heart's desire? Well, it probably began with a thought, but this was not just any old thought. In the very moment of the thought's conception, you put your heart into the matter ... get it? Your heart energy joined with the energy of your thought, creating a powerful combination and manifesting a truly heartfelt desire.

Have you noticed that when you put the energy of love into your life, your life changes? Simple things like smiling at people, being nice, enjoying a song, appreciating the beauty of nature, loving your job, home, spouse, and friends, giving unexpected presents and see-ing the joy in the face of the recipient, watching your children grow, reading a good book, being thankful for the gifts in your life—all these things have your heart in them. Well, putting your heart into the matter means exactly that.

Helen Keller said, "The best and most beautiful things in the world cannot be seen or even touched. They must be felt with the heart." Your heart is the center of love; it pumps the life force around your body. When you put your heart into the matter, you are putting love into it. When you love, the world loves you right back again. This is how you bring your wish to fulfillment. It cannot happen if you are only half-hearted. You must want it with all of your heart or not at all!

Which five-letter word, mentioned earlier, can be found in the word heart? Go on, move the letters round. What do you find? The answer is *earth*. Each one of us is deeply connected to the earth; in Greek mythology it is known as the mother, or Gaia. We are the keepers of this beautiful garden, which is uniquely reflected in all of our hearts. The increase in the earth's seismic activity appears to be a reflection of our own emotional development. In the last century, the emphasis has been upon changing our hearts and clearing them of unwanted emotions, using therapeutic techniques such as psychotherapy and counseling. Is the earth also ridding herself of unwanted energy?

We are an extension of everything around us, both the visible and the invisible worlds. All matter is joined through the heart connection, which means that whatever is in your heart, whether it be love or fear, is attracted to you on an energetic level. Eventually this manifests into matter, including the things you want and the things you do not want. As you know, both will be made manifest in your life until you learn to control your ability to create, or more precisely, to influence the energy. When you make a wish, this is essentially what you are doing: affecting energy.

You are not powerless—quite the opposite, in fact. Learn to recognize how your inner world reflects your outer world. By knowing this you will understand why certain situations seem to follow you around wherever you go. One of the ways to remedy this is to put love into your life. I am not referring to romantic or material love. The kind of love I mean is a giving, generous, happy love, all-embracing and full of joy. It is the experience of harmony, alchemy, and peace. We are deeply changed in its presence, glimpsing a different world: one without war or suffering, where there is no starvation, pain, or disease. A world full of love is a world without fear. This is unconditional love.

Unconditional love is in all the things you want to attract. Putting love into your life expands your energy, affecting not only your life but also the lives of those around you. You will begin to notice subtle changes, seeming coincidences. Eventually your ability to make your wishes come true will be so spontaneous that you no longer want for anything because your life will already be full of blessings. You will have attracted them to you by merit of your love. Asking with your heart will ensure that you get not only what you want, but also what you need.

I have always found that wishing with passion is even more potent when it is stated in present time. Time does not really exist, not the way we know it. The only time that exists is now; after all, there is no time like the present. So when you are making wishes, be sure to state everything in present time. As you should know by now, there is no point in asking for something to be in your future; the future does not exist. You are not there; you are here, and this is where your power is. If you wish for something to be in your future, it is energetically put at a distance and therefore will never become a reality. Also, do not give your wishes a time limit. Goals are wishes with a time limit on them. We are talking about making your wishes come true, not your goals. Although they appear to be one and the same thing, your goals often need more input, whereas wishes require detachment, as you will discover later.

WISH PRACTICE:
Pink Bubble Meditation

☆ ★ ★ ★ ☆ ★ ☆ ★ ☆ ★ ★ ★ ☆ ★ ☆ ★ ☆ ★

Your heart is the feeling center of your being. Connecting with it will enable you to link with your inner wisdom. In this meditation we will use two colors—gold, symbolizing wisdom and abundance, and pink, symbolic of unconditional love and receptivity.

Find a comfortable position, close your eyes, and do what you need to do to relax. As you breathe, visualize golden light entering and filling your body and forming a shape within your heart. This shape is the expression of your heart and will appear in a form that is easiest for you to accept. It might be the shape of a friend, loved one, or maybe someone you admire; it could even be formless. Just allow it to be whatever it needs to be in this moment. Take some deep breaths and synchronize your breathing with your heart's expression. You have made this wonderful connection, and your heart is ready to share with you.

Ask your heart questions about its feelings, what gives it passion, or how to make your wishes come true. Trust that your heart will give you exactly what you need at this time. Be aware that as you make this connection, a beautiful pink bubble of light is embracing you. How does it feel to be embraced by the light of unconditional love? As you bathe in this energy, visualize your wish using all of your senses. Put yourself into the picture—imagine your surroundings, the people, the weather, where you have been, and where you are going. Visualize your wish being granted and the excitement this entails.

Bring feelings of happiness, gratitude, and acceptance into your picture. Really get a sense of the fulfillment of your wish, allowing its essence to completely intoxicate your being. Breathe this wonderful feeling you are experiencing into your heart, and as you breathe notice the exchange of energy between your heart and the picture of your wish.

The pink bubble that has embraced you now begins to float like a balloon into the sky, carrying your wish with it, floating higher and higher until it reaches a star and explodes into tiny sparkles, forming a golden shaft of glittering light. This golden light stretches through space, comes in through the top of your head, and enters your heart, acknowledging that your wish has been granted. Give gratitude with the energy of your heart, and ask your heart to communicate one word to describe how it feels upon receiving this wish. Remember this word. Allow the visualization to fade away, and gently come back to waking consciousness.

As soon as you are back in your body, record your experience, feelings, and heart word in your wish journal. Use this word to create an affirmation. An affirmation is a positive declaration stating that you already have something in your life. Create a positive statement focusing on the successful culmination of your wish together with the feelings you experienced during the meditation. Include any relevant words you may have highlighted in your wish journal. Affirmations use positive words and are in present tense. For example, if my heart communicated the word *abundant* with me, my affirmation would be "I am living my life abundantly" or "I am abundant." If you get stuck, use the following example as the basis for your affirmation: "I am a wonderful, generous person who is open to receiving ... [insert your desire] ... in my life."

✫ ★ ★ ✫ ✫ ✫ ★ ★ ✫ ✫ ✫ ★ ★ ✫ ✫ ✫

Jennifer, a client, had not been in a relationship for at least two years, so her wish was for a man to be a part of her life. She mapped out a list of qualities of the perfect guy using the Relationship Plan that I teach. (See chapter 8, Wishing for a New Relationship, to develop your own Relationship Plan.) As she did this, she visualized the different men she had been in relationships with, pulling their most redeeming qualities into her plan. As a consequence, instead of one man, Jennifer ended up with three. Her plan had been specific enough, but her imagination had created the men she had visualized as she wrote her plan. Each guy embraced most of the qualities she listed in her Relationship Plan, or in this case her Man Plan. Now she had to decide which one fit the bill. She chose to meditate and ask her heart what it most wanted. She received a clear answer from her heart, which helped her make the right choice. Meditation calms the mind and can help you to connect with your inner wisdom. This aspect will guide you toward the correct path.

WISH SENSE TIPS

1. Put your heart into the matter. Put your heart into your wish by loving the idea of it being a part of your life. Thought

combined with a pinch of heart energy makes a potent recipe. When you put your heart into the matter, you allow your thoughts to be focused solely on your desire and nothing else.

2. Use the one-word essence from your heart. Connect with your inner wisdom through your heart center meditation, or any other method that works for you to obtain the embodiment of your wish in one word. Use this word to create a wish affirmation. Repeat it verbally, write it on pieces of paper, and place it in areas where it will be seen. Make a tape recording and listen to it as often as you can. Remember, this word might not be your wish, but it embodies the essence of your wish.

3. Specify your wish in present time. It is called the present because it is where you will find your gifts.

4. Your outer world reflects your inner world. If there is something that is manifesting in your outer world that is not working for you, then look to the inner to remedy it.

5. Visualize the effect a wish will have on your life. If you can bring this into your present consciousness, then you are halfway to becoming a master wisher.

If you make a wish for something and it is not the right wish, you will undoubtedly get a feeling that you are not going to be fulfilled. Some years ago I made a wish for a new job in my field of interest, complementary medicine. A few weeks later, I was given the opportunity to consider two jobs, one a paid position and the other voluntary. I had difficulty deciding between them because money was an issue and I needed to have an income. On the other hand, the voluntary position was a wonderful opportunity. Finally, I decided to go with my heart and take the voluntary post.

As soon as I made this decision, my heart skipped a beat and I felt utter happiness. I discovered that even though I did not earn any paper money, my needs were met and I did not want for anything. In addition, as a consequence of going with my heart (and my wish), I received an abundance of blessings in my life, including meeting my husband.

The Fourth Principle: Wish Once

Wish once means making the wish one time only as opposed to constantly asking for it to manifest. Asking more than once for the same thing actually causes a delay! For example, in this age of technology most people are familiar with computers. If a request is put into a computer, it will eventually fulfill the order. However, repeatedly inputting the same request causes the system to slow down. This in turn creates a delay that could have been avoided.

By asking for something more than once, you not only dilute the energy of your wish, but you also show that you have no faith in your ability to manifest. Author Stuart Wilde tells us, "The Universe Law is impartial. It will give you anything you believe.... [But] if you think God is coming down to fix things for you, forget it. God is out playing golf." In other words, the only person responsible for your life is you. Whatever name you give it (God, a guardian angel, a member of your family, or the universe), a compassionate spirit is always watching over you. This benevolent spirit wants the best for you, but no one is going to wave a magic wand. You have a significant role to play in the manifestation process. You are the magician, the alchemist, and the creator, so have faith in your ability.

The people who have made wishes before and never saw results are generally those people who are attached to the outcome. They ask for something to materialize but do not allow the energy to grow. They are unable to let go of their request. Consequently, it cannot return to them. A boomerang, a curved flat piece of wood used by the Australian Aboriginals to kill prey, is able to return to its thrower due to its shape. But if a boomerang is not released to do its job, then it cannot return. Instead, it stands inert. The same is true with wishes. Attachment is a form of fear; it is the fear of letting go. We are afraid to let go for fear that the opportunity will never present itself again.

Everything is a part of you, despite the apparent separateness, so as you align to the energy of your wish, the universe blesses and delivers it right on cue. It is important to practice patience; this is a sign that you trust your wish has already been granted. When you are infinitely patient, you are allowing the universe to do its work, resulting in a much faster outcome. Detachment from results frees you; otherwise you will be looking at your watch and waiting for your wish to manifest. Be unconcerned about how and when you will receive your wish. It may come at any time, in any place, and might not even appear to be what you had originally asked for, but never doubt that you will receive the essence of your wish.

Thinking about this on a practical level, buses do not always run on schedule, as we who use them frequently know. Whenever I want to catch a bus, I make a wish before I reach the bus stop, asking for the bus to get there a few minutes after my arrival. I visualize this happening by picturing myself arriving at the bus stop just as the bus is approaching. Next, I visualize myself getting on and finding a seat. Then I let the picture go, in total trust that my bus will be there as I had envisioned it. And it usually is.

This is not just limited to buses; the same thing can be achieved with any form of transport. It is particularly effective when you are running late and think that you will not be in time to catch your train or plane. Always remember to let go of the fear that you will not be able to get there in time. Fear blocks results.

There are times when it is for your highest good not to catch the bus or get what you want. This again can be a part of the greater picture. Or it may be that something you most want is not available at that time, or that all the pieces are not in place for your wish to show up.

Alternatively, if you drive a car, practice your ability to get a parking spot. Visualize the parking spot and see yourself driving into the space, parking perfectly. If it is busy, visualize a space being vacated just as you arrive. Ultimately, you will begin to appreciate how you can best do this for yourself. Work on it. If at first you do not succeed, try again until you do. When you get it right, look back on how you achieved the result. You can also try getting theater tickets for sold-out shows, an available cashier in a supermarket with long lines at each aisle, or an appointment at your favorite beauty salon when none are to be had. Always say thank you for every blessing that enters your life.

Just because you do not get what you wish for does not mean that you are making the wrong wish or that you are asking for it in the wrong way. A friend recently told me that he always visualizes parking spaces and usually gets one. When on occasion it does not work, it is usually because there are none available. He does not take this personally; he just accepts that everyone has to share a limited number of parking spots. If everyone is wishing for parking spots and there are only so many offered, then some will undoubtedly end up parking farther away from their destination than desired. There are a multitude of reasons this can happen. Maybe they had to meet someone on the way, or as a result of the frustration they felt at not finding a spot immediately, an emotion would come up that they needed to be aware of, or they could do with the exercise, or someone was meant to pass by their car and receive some of the healing energy they had left. Either way, remain detached from the outcome.

Of course, there is no point in asking for something when you are not ready or open to receive. If you ask for a relationship, be willing to receive it. If you request a new job, be prepared to take on the work. And if you wish for money, be ready to seek financial advice. Sometimes we ask for things to be a part of our lives, and yet we are not prepared to accept them. At other times everything falls into place so quickly that we have no idea if we chose this as our reality or if it chose us.

The universe has a tendency to know when you are ready, even if you are unaware of your readiness. Hence, you will discover that when you wish for something and it manifests, the universe is acknowledging that you are prepared, even if you think you are not. If you wish for something and it does not materialize, maybe the universe recognizes that you are not ready yet. This helps you to understand why some wishes manifest promptly whereas others can take longer to materialize.

This leads into another important factor. Acting as if you have already received your wish creates an energy that needs to be fulfilled. This does not mean that you can go out and spend lots of money because your wish is to win a million dollars. It signifies that you know you deserve it, and there is absolutely no question about it being yours. The universe has received a request, and while awaiting fulfillment you are claiming the space. "Believe it to conceive it!" and it will be so. This is what the Hebrew word *amen* means after a prayer. It translates as "let it be so."

Manifesting Your Wishes

Go back and read the short section on how to wish for the timely arrival of a bus or getting a parking space. This is a good way of practicing both your ability to manifest and your power of detachment from results. It will also help you to gain insight into your own way of manifesting wishes. If you want to try this, give yourself plenty of time and do it before you are due to catch the bus or go to the restaurant. Know with all of your heart that you will achieve your wish just as you pictured it. Remember to be realistic—you cannot stand at the bus stop in the middle of the night when there are no night buses and expect the bus to materialize out of thin air. Work on this; make it a regular part of your routine. Eventually your talent for making buses or parking spaces appear just when you want one will become your trademark.

Every morning my neighbor Terri bought coffee for both herself and her boss. The café where she purchased the coffees was so busy that it often took her twenty minutes to get the order in. It also didn't help that she was petite and tended to be engulfed by the crowd. One morning she decided to use her ability to visualize a positive outcome. On the train to work she visualized the crowd inside the coffee shop parting just as she entered, allowing the person behind the counter to see her and immediately take her order. Once she had put energy behind the image, she let it go. To her surprise this is exactly what happened. The crowd parted, the server saw her, and before she could think about what had occurred, two coffees were in her hands.

Terri decided to tweak her wish. She gave it a little extra time by visualizing it the day before she wanted it to happen. Again, she imagined walking into the coffee shop, saw herself walk up to the counter, immediately get served, and effortlessly walk away. The following morning when she walked into the coffee shop, she was amazed to find no one waiting to be served. Terri's reality mirrored her visualization in every way. She had no expectations of how it was going to manifest; she just let go of the image and was open to receiving her wish in whatever shape or form it may take. This story is a good exercise in simplicity and a perfect example of how wish sense works.

WISH SENSE TIPS

1. Ask once. Continuing to ask shows that you have no faith. Ask for your wish once. Put all of your energy into it, and then let the wish go.
2. Detach from the outcome. Attachment is a form of fear, and fear blocks results.
3. Be open to receiving. Your wish could arrive at any time, in any way, shape, or form.
4. Be patient. Know that you will receive the essence of your wish.
5. Believe it to conceive it! Know that you deserve to collect. Act as if the wish has already been granted.
6. Exercise your visualization muscles. Practice your visualization techniques to obtain parking spots, etc. Once you have perfected your technique, there will be no stopping you.

Once you realize that everything is a part of you, this generates a sense of unification and harmony with the rest of the known world. It also helps you to understand how your thoughts, as energy, will either allow or prevent you from achieving your wish.

One of the most important things to remember in wish sense is believing in your own ability to manifest. There is a blueprint of you in every cell of your body called DNA. Imagine for a moment that you are the DNA of God, or whatever you imagine is the divine principle of existence. All the information required to create you is within your DNA. This would mean that all the information needed to create God is within you. Murdo MacDonald-Bayne, a British visionary and author, said, "The law is—when energy is encased in its smallest space it is then at its greatest intensity." He meant that the power of the universe is within each of us awaiting our awareness. Just as a bonsai tree has the potential to be approximately one hundred times its size, so we have the capacity to create more than we can ever imagine.

The Fifth Principle: Wish Gratitude

Normally, when you give thanks you are using words to show your gratitude for a kindness done unto you. For instance, when someone opens a door or gives up a seat, when you receive a compliment or an unexpected gift, when someone shows appreciation of you, or when you are told that you are loved—these are gifts willingly presented to you in appreciation of your existence. But what about the world you live in: do you regularly give thanks in honor of its gifts? Do you give thanks when a flower opens, when the sun shines, or when a tree protects you from the rain? Do you say thank you when the traffic lights turn green just as you are approaching? How often do you appreciate the blessings in your life? In Vicky Wall's book *The Miracle of Color Healing*, she has a beautiful line about her walk through an avenue of trees. She says of the trees, "I would bless them as I passed, and was blessed by them."

You may think that a traffic light turning green just as you are approaching it is an accident, but how can it be when you are the creator of everything in your life? Remember how the cat wanted to stay warm? The cat had a desire for warmth and, against the odds, attracted to it the means to create this reality. Well, traffic lights are on the same level. You attract to you the light turning green, allowing you to keep moving instead of coming to a standstill. This desire, like the cat's, can change the mechanical synchronicity and can work to your advantage.

It is important to appreciate the world you live in, and having an attitude of gratitude includes the challenges as well as the gifts in your life. Now, why should you be grateful for the challenges? Certain situations appear to serve no other purpose than to create pain. We give our power away by imagining ourselves as helpless victims of a cruel world. But not everything in this world is as it appears!

Imagine that you could feel no pain. How would you be aware that something was wrong with your body? How would you know you were burning yourself every time you cooked? How would you recognize that someone was being cruel to you? Pain is a warning sign that something is wrong. It serves a purpose, as does everything else in your life. Although the reasons for it may be elusive, recognizing the meaning of its presence is up to you.

Deep pain and suffering can make you pull out all the stops. They can help you to reassess your life and turn it around. They can teach you to stand up for yourself and help you out of a rut. Without pain you would have no empathy for those in the world who suffer poverty, disease, and violence. It is only in our darkest moments that we can see the greatest light. In essence, the pain can show you a different way of life.

The universe resonates with the beautiful energy of gratitude. Just imagine how you feel when you give to someone unconditionally and they honor you by saying thank you. Doesn't it make you feel happy to have made a difference in someone's life? What if you were thanked for everything you did? As soon as you leave the house, the mailman thanks you for having mail, the bus driver thanks you for getting onto his bus, the person you sit next to thanks you for sharing your energy with them, the waiter thanks you for allowing him to serve you, the shop assistant thanks you, your boss thanks you, everyone you work with thanks you, and so on.

Take this a step further and imagine that all inanimate objects also appreciated your presence. The radio you turn on in the morning, the chairs, tables, the fridge, sink, your car . . . if everything in your life thanked you for just being there, imagine the elation; imagine how wonderful you would feel to be alive.

This is exactly how the universe or the energetic vibrations of your environment respond when you appreciate everything in your life. It shows that you are accepting responsibility for your ability to manifest while acknowledging the part the universe plays in this process. Appreciating what you have means that more will come to you. It is all about energy. If your predominant thought is that you do not have enough in your life, then this is what you will attract: a state of lack. If you think someone else has a better life than you and you want their life instead of your own, then you are not putting enough energy into your life—again a state of lack. You will only get what you put out, and that is why it is so important to have an attitude of gratitude. This then sets up another kind of energy, which attracts wonderful things into your life. Remember to say thank you for all the blessings in your life, especially since everything is a part of you, so when you say thank you, you are really honoring yourself.

It is also important to treat what you have with love. How can you expect anything better if you do not treat what you already have with the care and attention it deserves? This goes for people, too. Treat them with the love and respect they deserve just as you would expect them to treat you in return. If you want something better, then start treating what you already have with appreciation. Everything around you is an extension of you and what you believe about yourself on a deep level. Appreciating what you have will not only make you feel happier but will attract more of the same abundant energy into your life.

Although you may not have received your wish yet, give thanks to the universe for giving you exactly what you need. Having an attitude of gratitude for everything in your life will improve your chances of receiving blessings. You are affirming to the universe that whatever you have wished for has your name on it and will be accepted into your life in whatever shape or form it may appear. Always give thanks both before and after making your wish. It shows that you are prepared to take that leap of faith required to achieve the fulfillment of your desire.

One of my clients recently told me that she had embraced an attitude of gratitude and it had changed her whole way of being. It lifted her energy and enabled her to see the joy in life, even the joy in the challenges of life. Merely giving a compliment to others can make their day and change energy. This change can result in something wonderful happening.

WISH PRACTICE:
A Celebration of Life

★ ∗ ★ ∗ ☆ ∗ ∗ ★ ∗ ☆ ∗ ★ ∗ ☆ ∗ ∗

For today and every day . . .

1. Think of those you have not thanked but wanted to. Make their day by telling them now.

2. Do something nice for someone, but do not tell anyone about it. You do not need recognition for your good deeds.

3. Tell three people how much you love them. It is often easy to find one person, but three can sometimes be trickier. If it is easy to find more than one person, then congratulations to you!

4. Give someone a compliment, and do not expect one in return.

5. Make a point from this day on to say thank you for everything in your life. The best time for this is in the morning before you start your day and before retiring to bed at night, like a prayer. This includes the negative as well as the positive aspects of your life.

It can be more of a challenge to really be grateful for the negative, but eventually you will begin to appreciate why certain things happen to you, and this awareness makes it easier to be thankful. Instead of acknowledging the negative aspects of your life as negative, value them as challenges. The same with the positive aspects—recognize them as gifts.

Make a record in your wish journal of how this day made you feel. Schedule a regular appointment with yourself at least once a month to celebrate your life in this way. You will not only feel better for it, but you will begin to appreciate that your life is already abundant and full of blessings.

☆ ⋆ ★ ⋆ ☆ ⋆ ☆ ⋆ ☆ ⋆ ★ ⋆ ☆ ⋆ ☆ ⋆ ☆ ⋆ ★ ⋆ ☆ ⋆ ☆ ⋆ ☆

WISH SENSE TIPS

1. Have an attitude of gratitude. Appreciate everything in your life. Like attracts like, so appreciate the blessings in your life—the challenges as well as the gifts. The more grateful and appreciative you are of what you have, the more of like energy you will receive.

2. Treat everything you have with love. Remember to include yourself.

3. Say thank you both before and after you receive your wish. This means that once you have made your wish, thank the universe for granting it. Once it has manifested, thank the universe again. A wish does not just happen to you; you are in partnership with the universe and taking an active role in its manifestation.

4. Celebrate your life. Whether you believe it or not, you have consciously chosen to take part in the game of life. So do not take yourself so seriously; enjoy your life. As the saying goes, "angels can fly because they take themselves lightly!"

I always feel good when I say thank you to others because I am acknowledging appreciation for their existence. They are not necessarily concerned with making me happy, but the effort they have made makes me feel happy and valued. I cannot imagine a world without the words *please* and *thank you*, and can only suppose that it would be a sad world indeed if they were not a part of our language and culture. And yet, words are not all we have to show our appreciation; the way we look at someone, our demeanor, our way of being, or just a smile can show more than words can ever say. These gestures express how we feel, and this can mean more to someone than empty words.

The Sixth Principle: Wish-Tell Spell

This is where the rules of wish sense fall into your own hands. When making a wish, you have to decide whether it would be in your better interest to tell someone about it or to increase the energy by keeping the wish to yourself. Here are some examples:

A friend of mine recognized from an early age that she had an amazing ability to manifest anything she wanted in her life. At the time of this incident, she was unfortunately living on the streets of London, and it never occurred to her to manifest a home. Later in life she became a millionaire, all through the power of her own thought. She was a music lover and portable CD players were all the rage. She had seen the young kids walking around with them and did not want to be left out. So one morning she made it her intention to acquire a portable CD player and conceived a silent wish. By the end of the day, she had accumulated no less than five players, all in working order and all by honest means. So strong was her belief in the power of thought that she was rewarded not once, but five times.

How did she manage to get exactly what she wanted in such a short space of time? She made a point of telling people what she wanted, and they in turn helped her to realize her wish by becoming a part of her reality and producing the desired object. You do not have to do this, but sometimes the person you instinctively tell has exactly what you want. In my friend's case, this amounted to five people who were more than willing to help out.

I remember deciding that I needed to have a cell phone, although I had resisted the trend for a long time. However, I had spent half my life moving not only from home to home, but from country to country, too! My friends and family were exasperated by my nomadic lifestyle, but their main complaint was the number of pages I had used up in each of their address books. So I thought it high time I invested in one telephone number. Later the same day I visited a friend, who on hearing of my resigned decision offered me his phone—a very generous offer and one that surprised me. At that time I realized my ability to manifest, but this had happened so quickly—within the space of half an hour—that I was taken aback.

Things happen that quickly. Once you make a habit of wishing and receiving you will never want again. Eventually, in an ideal world, your wishing thoughts will create spontaneously. Then the saying "be careful what you ask for because you just might get it" really will be operative. Some wishes manifest even when we no longer want them. At the time the wish was made, it was something that was wanted and had enough emotion behind it to create it.

For instance, I made a wish to appear on a particular television show in England. I imagined what I would talk about, how long my slot might be, and how often I would be invited back on the show. I made no attempt to follow through with my thought and put it aside as a distant dream. Six months later I was asked to appear on the program when the company I worked for received an invitation from their research department—although by this time I had changed my mind about appearing on the show. It had been a mere flash of inspiration, a brief thought in time, but obviously with enough energy behind it to manifest. It goes to show that once the wheels are set in motion, your wish will eventually come into effect.

Generally, when you wish for something there has to be positive intention and energy behind the wish. The occasional thought will not manifest unless there was a desirous energy at the time of the thought. Our minds are active most of the time. While some thoughts are mundane, others involve making plans and expanding on our dreams. These are often the ones that come with heart energy and can evolve into a manifested wish.

There are some instances when it is not in your better interest to share the contents of your wish; some wishes are best kept to yourself. These are usually personal, involving your deepest emotions, such as wishing for fulfillment, success, happiness, love, or inspiration. Although all wishes contain these kinds of feelings and emotions, the most personal wishes are the ones where you are asking for this to be a part of your life without it being the essence of another wish.

For example, if you wish to be a homeowner, this is the kind of wish you can share with another, as the intention behind the wish is to create a home. However, if you have lived in fear or felt unsafe and insecure in your life and your wish is to feel protected and safe, then this has a slightly different energy behind it. I call this a personal wish. It may be more about your feelings than about manifesting something physical. Of course, as with anything it is always best to use your intuition when making decisions.

If you intuit that someone can help you feel more secure, then share your wish with that person. It might be that the person you talk to is a therapist who can suggest ways of healing your fears, or maybe someone who owns a security business that can make your home and your life feel protected. Or it could be someone looking for a job as a personal security guard. Unless you are comfortable with sharing your innermost feelings with others, it can be more difficult to involve another person in your personal wishes. Sometimes, by keeping these kinds of thoughts to yourself, you can increase their power and thereby have a greater chance of drawing them to you. The saying "a problem shared is a problem halved" means just that. By sharing certain problems, the energy dissipates and does not hold as much power. Therefore, the energy of a wish will also disperse by sharing it, except when you instinctively feel the time is right to tell someone about your wish.

You are the only person who can decide whether it is in your better interests to share your wish with another. Use your own intuition. If it feels right, then communicate your wish with the person you intuitively know will be able to help you to achieve its fulfillment. Go with the flow and allow your inner self to tell you when and if the time is right for you to share your wish. But as outlined earlier, if it is a personal wish, it may be better to keep it to yourself.

Writing your wish can be a creative way of manifesting all the details. Words hold power, so writing your wish can be a compelling tool to make it more potent. Your words will increase the energy behind the wish. If you choose to do this, there are two rules. Keep it simple, and make it specific. If you stick to these two rules, you should not need any boundaries concerning the length of your wish. Again, there needs to be the energy of intention and desire behind it. Otherwise, regardless of how many times you write the wish, it will remain as words on a page.

Life Plan

An interesting exercise is to create a Life Plan, a proposed plan of certain aspects of your life, from your ideal career to shaping your personal life. I often advise my clients to write a Life Plan, usually with a time connected to it such as ten years' time or fifteen years' time. The idea is to write a plan of the kind of life you would like to have in a certain time. However, I also used this plan when I wanted to plan my work path with no thought of timing attached to it. I thought about the kinds of things I enjoyed doing. I wrote them all down and then looked for a pattern or for a common thread. Once I had that common thread, I started to plan what kind of environment I wanted to do my work in. I made a list of the perfect work setting. I made my wish, and three weeks later I was standing in the perfect setting for my work with the opportunity to begin a whole new chapter of my life.

WISH PRACTICE:
Life Plan

★ ⋆ ★ ⋆ ⋆ ⋆ ☆ ⋆ ⋆ ⋆ ★ ⋆ ☆ ⋆ ☆ ⋆ ⋆ ★ ⋆ ☆ ⋆ ☆ ⋆ ⋆

Let's take one aspect of the Life Plan and say you wish to plan your career. Take a blank piece of paper and write down everything you are good at, incorporating all the things you enjoy doing most. Include everything; this is a plan, not a résumé. When you have finished, look over your list and decide what kind of job you have created for yourself. Look for the common thread. Try not to judge this process. And forget the editing!

Once you have done this, imagine your ideal career and write a letter or a list specifying what kind of place you would like to work in, how it will be decorated, what the external environment should be like, the kind of people you will work with, if any, and any other specific details. Study what you have written and visualize it in your mind. Really see yourself in this picture, working and living your dream career.

★ ⋆ ★ ⋆ ⋆ ⋆ ☆ ⋆ ⋆ ⋆ ★ ⋆ ☆ ⋆ ☆ ⋆ ⋆ ★ ⋆ ☆ ⋆ ☆ ⋆ ⋆

The first time I wrote a Life Plan, I specified exactly what I desired in my life, including work, environment, and people. This was something I wanted with all my heart, and I was completely open to it becoming a part of my life. A short time later, I was pleasantly surprised to find that my Life Plan criteria were being fulfilled to the letter, although I had not expected it to begin quite so soon. I had made no expectations about how this could happen, nor had I concentrated on the practicalities of the plan. But when the opportunity arose, I welcomed it with open arms and said yes to the blessings being offered.

Part of my plan was a new career. I knew basically what I wanted to achieve, but I was unsure of which direction to take. Once I had written down all the things I enjoyed doing, I realized that my path was that of an educator, although at the time I did not have any qual-ifications to be a teacher. Despite this seeming obstacle, within months I was using my knowledge to tutor people on subjects that were close to my heart. You can do this for any aspect of your life. Try it and see what you come up with.

Showing that you are serious about your wish is one rule you need to remember. You can demonstrate this by taking a step toward it. There is a joke about a man who prays for divine intervention to help him win the lottery, and his God says, "I cannot help you until you buy a ticket!" Some wishes require that you take the first step toward them. Do not wait for a result to land in your lap. Sometimes you will be lucky, and it will take the least amount of effort. But if your wish can be helped along a little, then give it a nudge. If you want a new job, you cannot sit at home waiting for it to happen. Remember that energy attracts energy. Whatever you wish for, recognize that you are in partnership with the universe. You have your part to play, and the rest belongs to the universe. But the application form is in your slice of the equation!

My husband, Win, always tells me to ask for what I want. It is his personal motto. As a life coach, he sees many people who are looking for answers. One young lady he coached wanted to sing and play music. He asked her what was stopping her. She replied that she could not imagine singing without strumming a guitar, but she did not own one. However, she felt that if she did, it would give her the incentive to create music. Well, Win is a country-and-western fan and just happened to have a guitar that he did not use. He immedi-ately offered it to her. He told me that her whole being lit up. Even though she had not asked my husband for a guitar, she vocalized the wish that was in her heart, and he helped to manifest it.

When was the last time you participated in someone else's wish? They wanted something, and you had just what they needed. You did not want it anymore or realized their need was greater, so you gave it to them. Be aware of playing a role in other people's wishes. If you can help them, then do so, as this will set up a new energy.

You will discover that as a consequence you will be given help with your wishes in the same way. As the saying goes, "what goes around comes around."

WISH SENSE TIPS

1. To share or not to share: that is the question. Decide whether or not you would benefit from sharing your wish. This will reduce the energy of a wish, but the person you instinctively tell may have exactly what you need to help you to manifest your wish.

2. What goes around comes back to you. Participate fully in others' wishes if you can help them. Give to others, as you would like them to give to you.

3. Be careful what you ask for because you might get it! Become consciously aware of how you create your wishes.

4. Take the first step toward your wish. Do not simply sit at home waiting for life to happen to you. Be serious about your wish. If you can take a step toward it, then what are you waiting for?

5. Focus your energy. Writing your wish can help it to become more real and can help you to focus your energy.

The Seventh Principle: Wish Forget-Me-Now

John Lennon once said, "Life is what happens when you're making other plans." In other words, life happens regardless of what you do, and your wish will develop in just the same way. So the first golden rule is: forget about your wish. Do not put your life on hold waiting for your wish to come true. That is like living with one foot in the future. By keeping both feet firmly in the "present" moment, you will be more prepared to receive your "gift," often when least expected.

Dorothy Parker wrote a poignant short story called "The Telephone Call," in which she recalls her internal torment while waiting impatiently for her prospective boyfriend to call. It begins with an all-too-familiar sentence for anyone who has been in the same position: "PLEASE, God, let him telephone me now.... Please, please, please." Throughout the piece she goes through every kind of emotion: begging, cajoling, bribing, and even making promises to be a better person if her wish is granted. But all her pleas are to no avail.

Have you noticed that the telephone rings the moment you leave the house or office? When you return and check your answering machine, it has recorded the time of the call at almost the exact moment you left. The saying "a watched pot never boils" could, in this case, be replaced by "a watched telephone never rings"! It is a rule that follows one of the many universal laws stated earlier: "where attention goes, energy flows." Now, you could argue that this would mean the person from whom you await a call would inevitably ring because you are concentrating on that outcome. However, more often than not, you are not only concentrating on the outcome but also holding onto the thought. This becomes like a blocked drain that you have successfully unblocked by using a plunger, but then continue to keep blocked by leaving the plunger in place.

If you do not let go of your request, how is anyone supposed to know what you want? Also, in many cases, you repeatedly change the scenario in your head. If you re-create the wish over and over, then your desire is an indecisive, incomplete wish and holds very little power. So how do you rectify this?—by knowing what you want and, after making your wish, letting it go and allowing it to manifest. In some ways letting it go is equivalent to forgetting about it, but we never really forget. Letting it go means that you are happy with your creation and are no longer attached to it or to the outcome. From this vantage point, you can look beyond the outcome to a time when it is already a part of your life. To help me remember to let go of a wish, I often imagine Joey from the television comedy show *Friends* saying with his Sicilian drawl, "Forget about it!"

There is another energy that could prevent you from manifesting your wish—the energy of desperation or neediness. Unfortunately, desperation and neediness increase the more disheartened you become, which means that you will attract circumstances to you that make you even more anxious. Ironically, when you desperately want something it becomes the most elusive thing in the world to you. This is because you are emotionally attached to expectations, and attachment acts like an energy barrier that obstructs your wish. It is like holding on to something that you have had for years when it is no longer of any use to you, creating an energy that cannot be released.

If you are desperate for something to happen, it either never does or can take longer to manifest. Whether it is money, a relationship, or a fulfilling career, it can seem beyond your reach when you really want it to be a part of your life. How often have you heard people say that they met the love of their lives just when they least expected it, even when a relationship was the last thing on their minds? Some of the world's most successful people had their life-changing ideas when they focused on something entirely different. There are workshops and seminars available that are specifically designed to tap into the creative mind by making the participants think of something other than their goals, and yet they still achieve the outcome they most wanted.

Neediness creates an energy lock, and the key to wish sense is to detach yourself from the end result. Think about the times when you have really needed a bus. Did you clock-watch, count the minutes, watch the road constantly, or did you relax and have faith that the bus would come on time and get you to where you wanted to go? Have you noticed that as soon as you do not need a bus, three come in swift succession? Or when you are late for a meeting all the traffic lights are on red, and when you have plenty of time they are all on green? Even buses and traffic signals are subject to universal laws!

This does not always happen, of course, but the point is that when you change your relationship with the outcome, it can happen more often than not. And this is the law of letting go: detaching from the outcome and allowing the gift to come to you. Letting go accelerates results; being attached to it is an energy that holds it in place so there is never an outcome. If it is not released, then it cannot come to you. Let go of everything except for the wonderful feeling that your wish has been granted. Get on with your life and detach yourself from the end result.

Detachment allows the universe to provide for you. If you hold on to your wish, there will be no room in your life for its fulfillment. It will just be a dream. It could be minutes from manifestation and it could be years, but once you become adept at wish sense, the time between wishing for and receiving certain wishes will be reduced. Then you might call yourself an alchemist. Alchemy takes on many forms, but in this instance a true alchemist is someone who has power over matter and the knowledge to make anything attainable (matter is often thought of as referring to the mystical philosopher's stone, the subject of one of the Harry Potter books). As an alchemist you will fine-tune your creative power, and you will discover that many of your wishes can manifest immediately.

Neediness can prevent your wishes from manifesting. One way to let go of neediness is through gratitude. Start by valuing what you have in your life. Seeing the value in everything will help you to be thankful for how much you have right now. We often tend to wish for things that are already present in our lives, and that we have failed to notice.

Appreciate yourself and the people you surround yourself with. Appreciating yourself will allow you to comprehend that what you see as flaws are really gifts of love wrapped up in a different package. Appreciating those around you will allow you to be conscious of what you have created in your life. The clue is how they treat you. If they treat you with love, they are mirroring how you treat yourself. But if they treat you with contempt, then on some level you probably treat yourself with contempt. Your gratitude allows you to realize that everything you want is in your life right now. You just need a change of focus!

I believe that there is often a good reason that our wishes are delayed—we have created a safety valve. Imagine what the world would be like if your every wish instantly came true. Think back to when you were a child and all the wishes you made when someone was unkind to you. It would be an unhappy world if all our wishes became a reality. Your wish will come in the time it is supposed to come and in the way it is supposed to arrive. Just be open to receive, ready to be surprised, and trust that you have already done your part in making it come true.

WISH SENSE TIPS

1. Get on with your life. Things will come in their own time. The same goes for your wish—it will develop in its own time. While this is happening, get on with your life.
2. Be open to receive. Be kind to yourself; allow your wish to return.
3. Forget about it! Detach yourself from the end result. Know what you want, let it go, and then forget about it.

Throughout this book you have learned that thought is creative. You create everything in your life, including the "bad stuff." In this section of wish sense, you have discovered that you can have abundance in your life, provided you are not in a state of desperation about things you want or do not have. Letting go is a crucial ingredient of wishing. When you master this ability, you can have everything.

Part IV
Wish Fulfillment

You have your brush, you have your colors,
you paint paradise, and then in you go.

—Nikos Kazantzakis

7

The Wish Formula

Some people walk in the rain, others just get wet.

—Roger Miller

Now that you have learned how to manifest your wishes using the seven principles of wish sense, the crucial question is, how do you put all this information into practice?

To begin, you need to learn how your own unique powers of manifestation function. In order to do this, start with your simplest wishes, such as a night out on the town, a new gadget, or a new pair of shoes. This way you will have the opportunity to observe and perfect your skills of manifestation within a short period of time, since simple wishes such as these can be granted spontaneously. Not surprisingly, some of these simple wishes can easily be achieved by just going out and buying whatever item is on your wish list. Remember that wish sense works by attracting to you whatever you desire, so you may be buying the item, but if you use wish sense to achieve your desire, you will almost certainly find exactly what you are looking for.

Just by using the wish sense principles, you will discover that you do not need to buy things; they will just come to you. I was on my way home from a friend's house one cold wintry evening, wishing I had dressed more warmly, when I decided to stop and look in a shop window. It was a clothes shop, and the window display included mannequins wrapped in thick wool coats, hats, and scarves. I found myself imagining how nice it would be to have a woolly hat on my head to keep me warm. I let the thought go and continued on my journey. I was within fifty feet of my home when I noticed a black object at the bottom of the flight of stairs leading up to the front door. At first I thought it was an animal, but on closer inspection I realized it was a piece of cloth. When I picked it up, I was surprised to find a brand new woolly hat in my hands, exactly like the one I had seen in the shop. No one in sight, and there were no clues to the owner. I called my friends, but none of them laid claim to the hat; it had manifested out of nowhere—as usual!

Whenever I lose something I know that it is just part of an energy exchange and maybe it needs to go to someone else, or it is time to let it go and I need to learn detachment. I am often aware of playing a role in someone else's manifestation process, even when I have no knowledge of to whom or where my lost item is going.

Your most magnificent wishes, such as a dream vacation in a tropical paradise, owning a successful worldwide business, or achieving superstardom in the greatest picture ever made are more complex and may take a little longer to achieve. The next chapter will help you to deal with these sophisticated wishes. A less tangible wish, such as a new way of being or attaining peace and love in your life, can be either a simple or a complex wish and largely depends upon your capacity to be open to receiving the heart of your wish. Many people have grown up with the idea that it is better to give than to receive. As a result, the receiving part of our being may be a little out of practice. This is also addressed in the next chapter.

For now, try this short exercise. Stand up with your feet shoulder-width apart. Take a deep breath in, and open your chest up by lifting your arms at right angles to the body and taking them back as far as they will go, while at the same time pushing your chest forward. You can add to this by tilting your head back and closing your eyes. Now repeat three times, either aloud or in your mind, "I choose to be open to receiving the love and abundance of the universe." Say thank you, and let go of the position.

Meanwhile, to begin with, it can be more rewarding if you focus on a wish for something modest rather than something that could drastically change your life.

Wish Directory: Four Wish Intentions

To make things easier, I have created a wish directory, designed to help you to prepare, organize, and create your wishes. The directory includes the main points of each chapter and the exercises from previous chapters that you can use to achieve your wish. It begins with a Four Wish Intentions exercise, akin to the four directions of north, south, east, and west. While you do not have to go through these Wish Intentions every time you want to make a wish, they can confirm whether or not you are making the wish for the right reasons and if it will be hindered by influences from your past.

Go through each Wish Intention in sequence, and if you discover that you are asking for the wrong thing, either change the wish accordingly or choose another wish and begin again. Some of the Wish Intentions may appear repetitive. They are just homing in on your wish from a different perspective and are designed to guide you toward your true wish.

Preparing Your Wish

First, decide on your wish. It is often best to start simple and then work your way up to something more substantial or adventurous. You can imagine it to be like baking a cake: it's best to start by making cupcakes rather than a multi-tiered wedding cake. If you decided to take up sailing, it's probably better to choose a small boat to begin with than a yacht. A simple wish would not have the emotional impact on your life that wishing for a new relationship would. A simple wish might be the bus arriving on time, getting a parking spot, someone bringing you a cup of coffee, that kind of thing. Start simple and work your way up.

The Wish Intentions are aligned with the Native American symbolism of the Four Directions, starting with east representing vision.

Wish Intention One: East/Vision—Why do you want this in your life? Use the Why exercise in chapter 2 to help you to discover why you are making this wish. Remember that the outcome of this exercise may reflect what you are really wishing for, the motivation behind your wish.

Wish Intention Two: South/Creation—Why and when did your need for this originate? Use the Nondominant Hand exercise to find the initial stimulus. Discover the origin of your motivation—if it is out of habit, if it was a belief that is no longer relevant or was never true, or if it is a true wish. If the Nondominant Hand exercise does not work for you, then try the meditation instead. You can use the result of the Why exercise here, or you can just look at the motivation behind your original wish. Both roads lead to the same destination.

Think about what your vision is of this wish. Ask yourself the following questions: What do I want? Why do I want this? Use Wish Intentions One and Two to delve deeper into why you want this in your life at this moment. For instance, if you are wishing for something simple like a cup of coffee, then maybe the why will be that you want to be respected and, in your eyes, having someone bring you coffee is a reflection of that respect.

Wish Intention Three: West/Adaptation—Which phase of life does your wish reflect? Use the Life Phases keywords to ascertain the nature of your wish. Alternatively, you can intuit by asking your inner self when this began, if it was not obvious, using the previous Wish Intention. Be open to the wisdom of your inner self, even if it does not immediately make sense to you. When you ask you can receive, but you have to ask first.

Wish Intention Four: North/Manifestation—Will this wish make a difference to your life? Answer these three questions without intellectualizing them:

> *What difference will this make in my life?*
> *Is this in my life now?*
> *Is there a truer wish I could be making?*

If this wish is not going to make a difference to your life, then maybe it will not have the energy behind it to manifest. The same goes for if this is already a part of your life. We sometimes make wishes for things that are currently in our lives. This does not mean that it will not manifest, although it could have a bearing on the outcome. Finally, you may come up with a yes for the final question. If you do, then determine if the truer wish is based upon your current wish or if it is a different wish altogether.

Organizing Your Wish

Organizing means placing things in categories or in sections. Wish Intentions One and Two prepare the motivation behind your wish. Again, if we think of this as baking cupcakes, then it means that the previous Wish Intentions have placed the approved ingredients in front of you. Now all you have to decide is what you are going to do with them and where those ingredients are going to be used. Wish Intention Three asks you to take a look at which phase your wish relates to. For the cup of coffee example, if this is about respect, then the phase could either be adolescent when the teenager wants more freedom, or the adult phase. If it comes from the adolescent phase, then you would have to be aware of the power struggles associated with this time of life. If it comes from the adult phase, the power struggle is still there, but is possibly less obvious and could be less reactive.

Creating Your Wish Intention

For the cup of coffee, let's say that you want respect, and are motivated by an adolescent need to be seen as well as respected. Wish Intention Four gives you support with this objective—if it is the right choice for you at this moment, if it is already present in your life, and what difference it will make to your life when it manifests. These are important questions even for a small wish like having someone bring you coffee. Knowing the answers will help you to formulate the kind of wish that will manifest in the way you want it to. This fourth Wish Intention helps you to create your final wish, somewhat similar to having all the ingredients in front of you to make those cupcakes— you have put them in the bowl and they are ready to be mixed.

Creating Your Wish

Your unconscious mind is a powerful instrument awaiting your instructions. When you eventually make your wish, you will be affirming its manifestation in your mind. Therefore, it is a waste of time making a wish that your mind believes is unattainable. Consequently, it will be to your advantage to shape your wish in a way that your mind will accept, understand, and agree with. In order to do this, write your wish on a piece of paper and work through the following suggestions. Some of the suggestions will help you to develop and improve the finer details of your wish, whereas others offer an optimum way of being during the wish sense process.

1. Use positive words.
2. Magnetize your wish by being optimistic and confident about its manifestation.
3. If you don't like the movie, change the picture. Use the Stepping Out meditation in chapter 4 to transform any unsuccessful areas of your life that could hinder the manifestation of your wish.
4. Fake it till you make it!
5. Ask yourself these questions:
   If this was in my life, what would it change?
   Am I ready for my deepest wish to come true?
6. Have a clear vision of what you want.
7. Love what you have.

If you are not ready, either you are making the wrong wish or something else is blocking your ability to be open to the manifestation of your wish. If you are not able to receive your wish, then it will pass you by.

Now you should be ready to make your wish . . .

The most important thing to remember in the wish sense process is to paint your picture in degrees. In other words, wish for one thing at a time, try not to make it too complicated, and be as specific as you can. Eventually, making a wish will only take you a few seconds.

A Simple Wish Example

Let's imagine that someone called Tara makes a wish for a new best friend, someone she can spend time, have fun, and share her life with. Going through the Four Wish Intentions she begins to ask herself, "Why do I want to make this wish?" She finds out that she wants a new friend because she feels lonely and craves companionship. Wish Intention Two then asks, "When did your need for this originate?" On the surface she might say that it is a recent wish, as she does not have a close companion at the moment. But going deeper into the question of where this loneliness originated, Tara discovers that it was created when her family moved from one home to another and she lost touch with her then best friend. Since that time she has never truly had a best friend. She decides that her loneliness is not a habit or a worn-out concept, but something that needs to be fulfilled now.

For Wish Intention Three she decides to ask her inner self, her inner wisdom, which phase of life her loneliness relates to. She realizes that it is part of the adolescent phase. This helps her to understand the kind of energy behind her wish and makes sense to her, as this was the time of life when she moved to another home. The questions in Wish Intention Four reveal that this wish would indeed make a difference in her life. She does have friends, but not a close friend. And finally, Tara decides that there would not be a truer wish to make, that a wish for a best friend is her true wish.

Now it is time for Tara to make the wish using the points from the previous section called Creating Your Wish.

1. Use positive words. Tara realizes that she has been somewhat negative about having a best friend and has focused too much on what she does not have in her life instead of what she does have.

2. Magnetize your wish by being optimistic about its manifes-tation. Changing her focus from negative to positive has made the prospect of a new friend exciting.

3. If you don't like the movie, change the picture. Using the Stepping Out meditation in chapter 4, she changes the energy around the move that her family made when she was a teenager and the feelings around leaving her friend behind.

4. Fake it till you make it! She imagines that her friend is away in another country, unable to get to a phone, with no email access, and not a mailbox in sight, but that she or he is send-ing energetic messages of love.

5. Ask yourself these questions:

If this were to happen in my life, what would it change?—For Tara this would diminish her loneliness and change her social calendar.

Am I ready for my deepest wish to come true?—yes, yes, yes! As she says these words, she opens her arms to invite her friend into her life.

6. Have a clear vision of what you want. She imagines the light at the heart of this person, not wanting to visualize a male or female, but just staying open to her wish's manifestation in whatever shape or form it may take.

7. Love what you have. She makes an intention to be more mindful of the friends she has and to share more time and energy with them.

Using the information gained from the exercises on paper, Tara's wish might look like this: I wish for a friend to share my light and life with, someone who lives close by, has similar interests to me, and is available to spend quality time and fun together. The image Tara has created matches the words and expands on the qualities she wishes to embody in her friend: light, life, quality time, fun, etc. All that is left is to go through the Seven Principles of Wish Sense.

Seven Principles of Wish Sense (Review)

1. Intention. This is your wish, the destination that guides the pathway of energy and action.
2. Focus. Visualize your wish in its entirety.
3. Want it with all of your heart. Affirm the essence of your wish in your life.
4. Ask once. Believe it to conceive it!
5. Have an attitude of gratitude. Say thank you both before and after your wish has manifested.
6. Do you need to share your wish? Use your intuition to guide you to the truth and the right person.
7. Let it go. It is now a matter for the universe.

Here is another wish with a little less emotional charge behind it. Let's say your wish is for a new pair of running shoes. Now, this may simply be a task of going to the local store and buying the brand of shoes that you know will fit. But what if you have difficulty finding the right fit and the right kind of shoe? This is where wish sense can help you. Going through the Four Wish Intentions, you start by asking, "Why do I want to make this wish?" By quizzing yourself you establish that you want a new pair of running shoes in order to feel comfortable. You are right-handed, so using your left hand to write the answers, you discover that your need originated when you were sixteen years old and you had a problem with blisters on your feet. Next, you take a look at the phase of life your wish relates to. It would seem immediately obvious that it relates to the adolescent time of your life. Asking the three questions in Wish Intention Four, you decide that you really want a pair of sneakers and, while you might have a few pairs, none of them are that comfortable.

As you move through the Creating Your Wish points, what strikes you is that you have always had difficulty finding sneakers that are just right. Point two asks you to be more positive, so you decide to be more optimistic about finding the right pair. The meditative process in point three takes you back to a memory of the first time you tried on a pair of sneakers. You had foot blisters at the time and each pair you tried rubbed against the blisters, making you feel uncomfortable. You decide to change the scenario during the meditation and replace this incident with a more favorable experience. You breeze through points four and five, but point six makes you conscious of not having a clear vision of your sneakers. You are aware that asking for a specific brand name is probably not such a good idea, so instead you decide to visualize what they will look like and how they will feel once they are on your feet. Point seven is easy. This is the basis of your wish. You want a comfortable pair of sneakers, and you love to be comfy, so there is nothing hard about that.

Finally, this is how your wish looks on paper—I wish to have a new pair of comfortable sneakers that fits perfectly, looks beautiful, and allows my feet to breathe. The image you have created matches the words and expands on their aesthetics: look, color, size, etc. The next step is making the wish using the seven principles.

WISH SENSE TIPS

I agree with the notion that time is just a thought we are having. When you wait for something, it seems to take a long time coming, but when you let it go, it comes along in no time at all. Here are a few words of advice when it comes to the earthly practice of timekeeping.

1. Limiting time limits you. Try not to give yourself a time limit—wishing is limitless. You might wish for something incredible that you think will take a long time to manifest and then be surprised by how quickly it materializes.

2. The power of now. If you are wishing in the present moment, and you should be, then in the universal scheme of things it is already yours.

3. Ask Once! Remember to ask just once—there is no point asking over and over again. It shows a lack of faith in your ability to manifest.

4. Sometimes wishes need time to grow. Expect your wish to be granted, but do not have any expectations about how it will manifest. If your wish is taking its time, there is almost certainly a good reason behind the delay. Allow your wish to grow in its own time and remember that everything happens for a reason.

8
Make Your Wish Come True

**Shoot for the moon. Even if you miss,
you'll land among the stars.**

—Les Brown

So far you have learned why you make certain wishes, whether or not they will manifest, and how to manifest them using the principles of wish sense. The wish directory in the previous chapter helped you to arrange your wishes in order of priority as well as to guide you through the various wish sense procedures. The example of the sneakers was a simple wish and easily attainable; however, complex wishes such as the wish for a best friend may require a little more effort on your part. For this reason, I have constructed the following sections in order to assist you with your wishes for a new relationship, a new job, more money, a promotion, a new home, good health, and a new way of being.

Wishing for a New Relationship

I have used this technique at various times in my life. The last time I used it, I met my husband. One client who applied the same system to attract a partner specified that her man should have a chiseled nose and long dark hair, work in the music business, and enjoy sports. Apart from these specifications she acknowledged that she wanted to have fun rather than a committed relationship. Instead of looking for her wish list guy, she realized that she had to create space for a relationship to come into her life. Hence, she took time off from her job, allocated time to go out with friends, and made having fun her first priority. Two weeks to the day after her wish, she met her wish list guy exactly as she had visualized him. Her wish manifested because instead of directing all of her attention to attracting a partner, she changed her priorities and let go of any expectations. Not all relationship wishes are quite so swift; some take longer than others, but having your wish granted is worth the wait.

Often, people assume that once they enter into a relationship their lives will change, but consider for a moment that each relationship is a mirror. Your soul has plans for its healing and attracts to it the relationships that will allow it to heal the unhealed parts of itself. Each mirror presents a picture of what you need to see about yourself in order to heal. This means that if you want something better, you have to change the reflection and not the mirror. For instance, if you constantly attract partners who are unfaithful to you, they may be reflecting your inability to be in an intimate relationship. Once you change this aspect of yourself, you essentially change your need for that particular reflection. As a consequence, either the mirror has to change also, or you will need to get a fresh mirror to enable you to see your new reflection—in other words, a new partnership.

Relationship Building Blocks

When you honor your values, you are honoring the qualities you place in your wish. Armed with this information, make a list of your values, identifying what is really important to you in your life. How do you live your life? Are you religious? Is it important to have honesty and integrity in your life? Look at how your friends treat you compared with how a partner treats you. Is there a difference? Once you have made your list, place your values in order of priority.

For example, my top priority value is love. This is closely followed by my spiritual life. I value honesty next and a sense of humor after this. The next step is to look down your list and compare your values with the kind of people you surround yourself with. For example, I am surrounded by people who are loving, spiritual, and honest, and who like to laugh. Relationships have to do with friends and family

and not just love partnerships. Are you honoring your values by surrounding yourself with people who embody these qualities? If not,
then what can you do today to change this? The answers should give
you a basic idea of what you really want in a relationship, your priorities, and what you have in your life right now.

Opening to Friendship

We often look for a relationship and don't understand why the ideal
person is slow to get the message that we are ready, or at least we
think we are ready. Another way to support you in this venture is to
try answering the questions below and see what comes up. Use a pen
and a piece of paper to write down your answers. Try not to edit the
answers or think about them too much. You want to be able to access
your wise self. To achieve this, it may benefit you to do a short meditation first to calm the mind. Play some soothing music to stimulate
your right brain and calm your left brain. That way, you will be best
prepared for this exercise. When you are ready, answer the following
questions immediately without thinking about them:

1. What do you most want from a relationship?
2. What is blocking you from having a relationship?
3. What kind of relationships have you attracted before?
4. What do you need to do in order for your ideal partner to
   show up?
5. What would change in your life if your wish were granted?

These questions may have opened doors to understanding why
this part of your life is unfulfilled. You can expand on question 3 by
making a list of your most significant love relationships. Include the
following questions: Why did each relationship begin? Why did
each relationship end? Is there a common theme? If there is a common thread and it is one that is not beneficial, then your deepest
beliefs or patterns may be contributing to the kinds of relationships
you are attracting. Psychology of Vision creator Chuck Spezzano

says, "Happiness is the best revenge." In his book of the same name, he says that revenge such as heartbreak is a form of hurting oneself to get back at someone else. Changing this can mean changing patterns and beliefs that have defined all those previous relationships. Seeking specialist help with a counselor or a psychotherapist can be beneficial. These professionals have ways of extracting information that you are unable or unwilling to reach on your own. They can assist you on your journey of self-discovery and help you to gain access to the deeper aspects of your makeup. Once you have accessed the obstacle that is blocking your relationship, you can initiate healing.

The five-question list should be one that truly reflects who you are and what you want in your life. Remember to identify exactly what you want. If you want fun, say so; if you want commitment, include this in your wish list. And do not forget to include the all-important magic word in your list: available!

Once you have transcribed your list of partner qualities, give it to a friend, someone who knows and loves you, and ask that person to add to the list anything he or she feels will enhance your life. It is important that you feel excited at the prospect of meeting someone who embraces all the qualities you have specified. It is also essential that you can visualize this person in your life. Finally, reread your list to ensure this is really what you want with all of your heart.

WISH PRACTICE:
Relationship Plan

✫ ✦ ★ ✦ ✫ ✦ ✩ ✦ ✫ ✦ ★ ✦ ✩ ✦ ✫ ✦ ★ ✦ ✩ ✦ ✫

First, prepare the way for your wish by constructing a wish list—a blueprint for a potential relationship. Essentially, you are organizing your relationship priorities by describing in detail your ideal partner and the kind of relationship you would like. Include in your list everything you desire in a partner: looks, body type, personality, career, hobbies, dress code, emotional state, romantic outlook, living situation, religion, beliefs, and so on. It is important not to specify a particular person; however, you can include qualities you admire in someone you know. Use the words in the wish box below to help you to formulate your list; circle the terms that best describe your potential partner.

Abundant	Cool	Good looking
Academic	Creative	Good listener
Accomplished	Cute	Handsome
Adaptable	Deep	Handy
Affluent	Demonstrative	Happy
Alluring	Devoted	Healed
Ambitious	Direct	High achiever
Animal magnetism	Domineering	Homeowner
Appealing	Easygoing	Honest
Approachable	Elegant	Humble
Athletic	Eloquent	Independent
Attentive	Energetic	Inspired
Attractive	Enthusiastic	Intense
Balanced	Exciting	Intelligent
Beautiful	Fair	Interesting
Buxom	Faithful	Knowledgeable
Calm	Family oriented	Learned
Candid	Fascinating	Liberated
Caring	Fiery	Lively
Charitable	Flash	Loving
Charismatic	Flirty	Loyal
Charming	Free	Manly
Chatty	Funny	Medium build
Clean	Generous	Mellow
Clever	Genuine	Moral
Compassionate	Gentle	Muscular
Confident	Good conversa-	Nice looking
Conventional	tionalist	Noble

Nonjudgmental	Rich	Submissive
Normal	Romantic	Supportive
Nurturing	Rugged	Sweet
Open	Sane	Tall
Optimistic	Selfless	Tidy
Organized	Sense of humor	Thoughtful
Passionate	Sensual	Trustworthy
Patient	Sexy	Truthful
Peaceful	Shapely	Unassuming
People person	Sharp	Uncomplaining
Philanthropic	Sincere	Understanding
Playful	Slim	Uninhibited
Powerful	Small	Vivacious
Pretty	Smart	Warm
Private	Social	Wealthy
Prosperous	Spiritual	Well-read
Quiet	Sporty	Well-rounded
Resourceful	Stimulating	Well-traveled
Relaxed	Straight	Wise
Reliable	Strong	Witty
Religious	Successful	Womanly
Responsible	Stylish	

Wish Words

As soon as you have finished, scan your list and place the qualities of your potential partner in order of preference. If looks come first, write this in the number one spot, if career is second, write this in the number two slot, and so on, until all of the qualities have been arranged accordingly.

Then, using a different color pen, circle the words that best describe you. When you have done this, arrange your qualities in order, just as you did for your relationship priorities in your wish list. Now, take your relationship priority list and reflect on what you would bring to the relationship by comparing it to your own list of qualities. For instance, if you have placed looks in position one, are your looks on a par with what you desire in a partner? In other words, have you put your own looks at number one? It is important to remember that you attract to you whatever you believe about yourself at a deep level. If you think you are attractive, but really believe you are unappealing, then this is the energy you communicate to the rest of the world. This energy is picked up by a potential partner who subsequently acts out a role that reflects your belief, albeit unconsciously.

It is a valuable exercise to look at all of your relationship preferences and to assess whether or not you come up to your own expectations of a partner. For example, if you placed career high on your list of priorities, look at what you would bring to the relationship. What kind of career do you have? Are you a good earner? Does your career come first? Are you all work and no play? These are important questions. It is unrealistic for you to expect something from someone else that you do not accept, appreciate, and nurture in yourself.

Once you have transcribed your list of partner qualities, give it to a friend, someone who knows and loves you, and ask that person to add to the list anything he or she feels will enhance your life. It is important that you feel excited at the prospect of meeting someone who embraces all the qualities you have specified. It is also essential that you can visualize this person in your life. Finally, reread your list to ensure this is really what you want with all of your heart. Use the wish sense techniques to take you further. One last note of advice: one of the major keys to a relationship showing up is to go about your life as normal. In other words, forget about it!

☆ ★ ★ ☆ ★ ✩ ★ ☆ ★ ★ ☆ ★ ✩ ★ ☆ ★ ★ ☆ ★ ✩ ★ ☆

The Relationship Plan is one of the most powerful aspects of wish sense, but it has to be used with integrity. One of my clients wrote a

Relationship Plan while still in a relationship, creating a bit of a situation when she manifested a new beau. Dissatisfied with her current partner, she wanted to see what would happen if she made a wish for a new one. The man she manifested had all the qualities of her ideal mate, or at least the qualities she thought she wanted. Meeting him made her realize that she was not ready to embrace her own qualities reflected in those he possessed. This experience provided her with a greater understanding of what she wanted in a relationship. It opened up her heart to her current partner and brought greater happiness into her life. Sometimes, just knowing that you have a choice will change energy around what you have in your life.

Wishing for a New Job

Recognizing what you want and knowing where you are going create opportunities, as illustrated by the amazing story of a British woman named Gladys Aylward. In 1957, Alan Burgess wrote a book about Gladys titled *The Small Woman*. Her incredible story was later made into a movie starring Ingrid Bergman called *The Inn of the Sixth Happiness*. Gladys worked as a parlor maid in London during the 1920s. She joined the China Inland Mission in London as a probationer after attending a revival meeting where the preacher had spoken of "dedicating one's life to God." She wanted to be of service by preaching the gospel, but she failed to pass the appropriate exams allowing her to go to China as a missionary. She then heard of an elderly missionary who needed a younger woman to continue her work in China. Gladys wrote to her and was accepted for the job—provided she could get there. Her journey was not an easy one. She traveled by ship, train, and donkey to get to the mission in the mountains of China.

The mission doubled as an inn for travelers, and the two women worked together to spread the word. When the older lady died, Gladys started to take in orphans at the inn. Once the war broke out, she knew that she had to get herself and the children to safety. One of her most remarkable feats was the journey she took with two hundred children during the height of the war. This involved walking for twelve days over mountainous terrain, sometimes without food and shelter, and including crossing the Yellow River to reach Siam, a safe haven. Without Gladys Aylward, these children would surely have perished. They did not care if she had the right qualifications to be a missionary. She had leadership qualities and the determination to succeed.

There is a well-known saying, "Where there is a will, there is a way." Gladys had a passion and knew exactly where she was going; in other words, she followed her heart. Ask yourself what kind of job you would do if you followed your heart. If you go with your heart, your intention will bring your desire into effect. If you want something, the universe will conspire to help you, provided you play your part.

The obvious question is what kind of job you would like. Unfortunately, not everyone has the answer to this question. If you do not know which direction to take, make a career list, an inventory of everything you enjoy doing. Include your hobbies and what makes you happy, what excites you, challenges you, and so forth. Once you have done this, read through it and imagine that you are a career adviser reading someone else's qualities. What kind of job would you advise them to take based on the list? Try not to get too caught up in the "yeah, buts"—"Yeah, but I can't do that because I'm not qualified" or "Yeah, but I can't do this because I don't have the money." Use your imagination and just for a moment imagine that you can have everything regardless of the cost and time.

Remember to play your part in this process. For example, an opportunity presented itself for Gladys to achieve her wish, and she took the next step by writing a letter to her potential employer. If your wish is to be a rocket scientist but all you have is a high school diploma, a way will present itself to allow you to achieve the essence of your wish. When you have decided what kind of job you want, look back at the Life Plan example and use this to help you to create a clear picture of your new work environment. Then go through the wish sense process to make it happen! Be persistent and do not give up on your dream. You have the creative power within you to manifest anything, and that includes your dream job.

Wishing for More Money

Money is a wonderful thing. It allows you to have whatever you want—or does it? We all think the grass is greener for those who have millions of dollars in their bank balance, but the truth is, money is energy like everything else in your life. First of all, let's transform your vision of money by calling it *abundance*.

Everyone has a different way of looking at how much abundance they have in their lives. For example, one lady who came to me for intuitive counseling began the session by telling me how broke she was. Yet she lived in one of the most affluent areas of London and had just purchased every woman's magazine available in the local store. I lived in the same area, yet I had very little money in comparison to this lady. My attitude was that I had plenty. That is why her idea of broke and my idea of broke were miles apart. Incidentally, broke is an interesting way to describe a lack of abundance; it explains perfectly how the energy patterns required to achieve wealth have been broken.

Abundance is a state of mind, as is scarcity. If you have a roof over your head, then you are abundant. If you can put food on the table, then you are abundant. If you have money in your pocket, then you are abundant. If you have friends, then you are abundant. Money is often called green energy not because of its color, but because abundance comes from the heart and heart energy is green. Therefore, increasing your heart energy expands your capacity to manifest and receive more abundance. Appreciation is energy, too. It comes from the heart and is one of the keys to greater abundance. Once you increase your appreciation, you enhance the odds of receiving more abundance. It sounds simple, but unfortunately we are complex human beings full of limiting notions that prevent us from being the abundant creatures we were meant to be.

Appreciating what you have allows the universe to give you more. There are numerous ways of showing your appreciation for the abundance you already have; one of these is to take responsibility for it. Throwing money away demonstrates your unreliability. If you do not use your money wisely, then you are attracting this erratic energy into your life. Consequently, you are always short of money.

Imagine for a moment that money is a living, breathing commodity. It has legs, arms, and a face and it can speak to you, embrace you, and work with you. It is happiest when it serves you, but it can only function when you have free-flowing energy. In other words, your capacity to attract money is highly dependent upon your ability to go with the flow. When you get stuck, so does money. Visualize for a moment a river of abundance flowing freely until your fears and limitations, symbolized by rocks, are placed in the river. What happens to the river? It becomes blocked and is prevented from flowing freely. Abundance works in the same way.

Giving to others unblocks the river of abundance. For example, a doctor in Mexico had just cured my client Pauline of a debilitating illness. She had spent almost all of her savings on her health, but it had been worth it. Shortly after her return to the United States, she met a woman who had fallen seriously ill due to an environmental allergy. Pauline believed that the doctor who had cured her could help this woman, but was dismayed to discover that her new acquaintance did not have the money to pay for the treatment. Pauline made the courageous decision to donate her last $1,500 to a virtual stranger in an attempt to help her to heal. Up until that point, she had feared the loss of her last few dollars, and yet she gave her money unconditionally. Fortunately, as soon as she did this, the energy of abundance began to flow freely. She was offered payment in part by two of the lady's friends. Her ex-husband offered her a lump sum of money—an offer that came as a complete surprise. Work picked up, and she soon made her money back, with interest.

"What you give out you get back" does not mean going on a spending spree. You will never be sent what you cannot handle. For example, begin to focus on the ways you give away your abundance. Do you buy things that are unnecessary? Do you overspend and put them on your credit card so that you are constantly in debt? Do you create situations that prevent you from being debt free? If you answered yes to at least one of these questions, then you lack appreciation for money and will therefore remain in a state of poverty consciousness, or lack of abundance. The way you treat money stems from a core belief. Healing the core belief can help you to regain your abundance. If you cannot manage the abundance you already have, then it is unlikely that you will attract more. Working with what you have shows that you know how to handle abundance. Being constantly in debt demonstrates your inability to care for green energy.

WISH PRACTICE:
Abundance

☆ ★ ★ ★ ☆ ・ ★ ☆ ・ ☆ ★ ★ ★ ☆ ・ ★ ☆ ・ ☆ ★ ★ ★ ☆ ・ ★ ☆ ・ ☆

Before attempting the following exercise, take some time out to relax, center yourself, and take a few deep breaths. Close your eyes for a moment and ask for the wise part of yourself to help you to answer the following questions. When you feel ready, answer the questions quickly with yes or no:

Is your core belief centered around . . .

1. Not being good enough to receive money?
2. Poverty consciousness?
3. Money is dirty?
4. Having money is not spiritual?
5. My parents did not have money so neither should I?
6. Money is the root of all evil?

If you answered yes to any of the above questions, then you need to establish where your core belief originated. The Stepping Out meditation in chapter 4 will allow you to discover the initial cause and help you to transform the scenario. If this does not work for you, seek the help of a counselor or hypnotherapist to discover and resolve the cause. Until you change your core belief, no amount of abundance will satisfy your needs.

The next step is to have a clear vision of your finances. Begin the process of balancing what you get with what you give out. Cut out any unnecessary outgoings, habits, or expenditures. By doing this you are proving that you appreciate what you have and using what you have with care and attention. As soon as you start to organize your finances, you will notice a shift in energy. Once this happens you are ready to make your wish for more abundance because you have proved to the universe that you are capable of handling it.

Go through the wish directory to help yourself formulate and stabilize your wish. It is important to wish for abundance and not for money—abundance incorporates everything. It is the source, whereas money is used to get you what you want. Visualize what you want in your life. How would your life look if you had more abundance? How would it feel to have all of your bills paid, to live an abundant life? Bring this feeling into your body, mind, and spirit—completely embrace yourself in the energy of abundance. Really get a sense of living your life abundantly on every level, and appreciate all the little blessings that are mile markers along the way. It is everyone's right to be abundant. Have some reverence for the energy of abundance. Treat it as a living being, like your best friend, and give gratitude for its presence in your life.

☆ ⋆ ★ ⋆ ☆ ⋆ ☆ ⋆ ☆ ⋆ ★ ⋆ ☆ ⋆ ☆ ⋆ ☆ ⋆ ★ ⋆ ☆ ⋆ ☆ ⋆ ☆

Money is an exchange of energy, yet therapists can often have the hardest time making money. This can be due to a belief that they have a gift and shouldn't ask for money, or that asking for money is not spiritual. Chris, a massage therapist, had difficulty attracting clients. She tried visualizing people coming into her room and being happy about the service she provided. That technique would work briefly. Then she tried telling friends about her business, asking them to pass along her contact information. This brought in a few people, but it soon trickled off. The most helpful part of wish sense for Chris was discovering where her issues around making money came from.

Beneath the surface Chris believed she was not good enough to earn money. She did not do well at school. She had been a sensitive child and found it hard to keep up with her studies. Because of her academic challenges her mother had told her that she would not amount to anything. This small statement was at the center of her inability to make a decent living. She felt that she was not capable of making money and therefore restricted her potential for abundance. Once she realized that this was preventing her from being successful, she made a plan of action. She used positive thoughts to change subconscious decisions she had made as a child. She stood in front of the mirror each day and told herself how gifted she was. She meditated on love, not just being loved or feeling it, but embodying the essence of love at her very core. She gradually began to see change in her life. When the changes appeared, she went back to visualizing clients and received an abundance of new clients to work on.

The well-known motivational speaker Tony Robbins realized the power of visualization. Each year he visualized a little more money coming in. The secret to making money this way is to visualize something your mind can accept. There is no point visualizing yourself earning a million dollars if your mind cannot accept it. Creating stepping-stones toward a wish will help to manifest it. This is exactly what Tony Robbins did. He visualized stepping-stones, a new one each year, until he reached and surpassed his goal. So you can ask for money provided you are not asking for it to get you what you want. Remember to ask for what you want, not something to get you what you want.

Wishing for a Promotion

Are you tired of being overlooked by your employers or peers? Do they habitually acknowledge less-experienced people? What are your thoughts on promotion? Are you the best person for the job? Wishing for a promotion has a similar energy supporting it as wishing for a new job, except when you wish to be promoted it is often within your own company. This can sometimes put additional pressure on you, especially if you are sensitive to the evaluation of your peers. Look at the reasons behind your desire for a promotion or recognition. Is it because you would like the opportunity to lead, have more respect, or have more money? A promotion is like a double-edged sword. On the one side it usually comes with more money, maybe a larger workspace, and more respect. On the other side it can mean longer hours, greater responsibility, and a commitment to remain in the position for a certain period of time. You will have to prove to the rest of the company that you can manage the added workload. Are you willing to take this on?

Promotions are not necessarily rewards for the best employee. They can often be political statements. Consequently, you may have lost out again and again to the favored candidate of the moment. Changing the way you look, being in the right place at the right time, or just buttering up your boss can have an impact on the promotional stakes. The biggest shift, however, will come with a change in your attitude.

External reality reflects your internal world. Therefore, if you are not getting what you want within your job, you need to change your attitude about ... the job! Changing your attitude about your work will either improve it or allow you to move on to a better job. Attitude is a way of thinking. If you think negatively about your work, then the energy you put out is unlikely to change anything. Consequently, nothing will change and you will remain where you are until you *change your mind*.

If you're not getting the recognition you want, you can change your attitude about ... you. Do you believe that you are good enough to get a promotion? If you do not believe at your core that you are good enough for the job, then neither will anyone else. Believing in yourself allows others to take your lead—energetically.

You can change your attitude about . . . your work colleagues. Relationships reflect what you believe at a deep level and can mirror something that you do not respect or like within yourself. For example, when someone consistently ignores your instructions, they could be reflecting your need to be in control. Getting rid of that particular person does not work because there will always be somebody else to reflect this aspect of your personality until it is healed. Fifty percent of healing is awareness. Therefore, when you understand why this is a recurring situation and make the intention to heal it, the reflection changes. Consequently, that person is either transferred to another department, changes jobs, or no longer acts in the same manner toward you.

You can change your attitude about . . . your workspace. Your workspace is a reflection of who you are and what you think about yourself on a deep level. Look around you. What kind of space have you attracted? What aspect of yourself are you showing to the world? Is it light and airy or dark and dismal? Is it full of garbage, items you do not need, and uncompleted work? If you do not like your workspace, you can make an intention to do something about it. Complete any unfinished business. Clear your space up. Add mirrors, plants, personal items, and color. Clear the energy with water fountains or crystals. Look at your space as a metaphoric reflection of who you are on a deep level, and begin to decipher the messages. Use visualization to connect with the wise space sage within—an insightful person who can help you to interpret the messages of your surroundings. Visualize this person as an interior designer who is able to tell you exactly what your space is reflecting. Once you become aware of what you are revealing to the world, you can take steps toward its transformation.

You can change your attitude about . . . your remuneration. If you are unsatisfied with your wage and talking to your employer about this has reached a standstill, then you may need to consider your relationship to abundance. Money will only manifest if you are open to receiving it. The previous section of Wishing for More Money may well clarify why you have been unable to achieve the abundance you desire. If a core belief is hindering your abundance, use the Stepping Out meditation in chapter 4 to ascertain its origin and to change the belief pattern.

Now, begin to connect with the feeling a promotion will give you, including all of the perks that go with it. For instance, a promotion might create more power, money, a bigger office, more responsibility, greater freedom, or even a key to the executive washroom. Whatever your promotion promises to bring, imagine that it is already a part of your life and embrace this energy in your life right now. Give it a name, a color, a smell, whatever works for you, and use this essence when you make your wish. Wishing for a promotion may change your position within your existing job, or you could manifest a completely new job. If you wish for a promotion and discover that you are about to lose your job, have faith that you have manifested this change and something wonderful is on the horizon, just as you wished. Either way, allow some time for your promotion to manifest completely. Some wishes take longer than others, and this particular one could manifest in stages.

A workshop participant named Jen had watched supervisors come and go at her firm. In spite of her lack of qualifications, she felt that she could do as good a job as any of them, if not better. She understood the power of wish sense and resolved to change her negative beliefs regarding her lack of credentials into positive energy. She also realized that she had to act the part. Imagining herself as the manager, she changed the way she dressed, tidied up her desk, and even walked in a different way. This energy change caught the eye of the recruitment manager. He called her into his office and asked why she had not applied for the vacant position. He listened to her explanation and said that he would look into the matter. That evening, much to her delight, he called her at home to tell her that, provided she was willing to go on the required training programs, she could take the position on a trial basis. Her wish had come true, and of course she jumped at the chance.

Wishing for a New Home

Sometimes I have driven through an area and thought how nice it would be to live there, but it was an area that cost an arm and a leg, so to speak, to live in. Regardless of the cost, I have consistently manifested a home in the area I thought of living. I have wished for apartments, houses, studios, rooms—with people or on my own—in the most salubrious areas of London, as well as other areas of the world, and they have always manifested, and just when I needed them. If I can do this, then so can you. We all have the capacity to manifest our thoughts, desires, and wishes.

It is easier to make a wish than it is to decide exactly what to wish for. The first secret to manifesting a home is knowing precisely what you want without getting too attached to the details. Use this step-by-step guide to help formulate your wish for a new home:

1. Have a clear vision of what you want. What kind of home do you want? Is it a house, apartment, condominium, chalet, cottage, villa? Visualize yourself walking from room to room. How many rooms does it have? What do the walls, floor, and furniture look like in each room? Where are the closets, and what do they look like? What shape are the windows? What kind of view does each room have?

   Once you have visualized the interior of your home, begin to explore the outside of it. What material is it made of? Is it made of stone, wood, brick, or siding? What color is the exterior? What does the front door look like? Are there steps up to the front door, or a pathway? What surrounds your home? Does it have a garden, a window box, a balcony, a deck, or acres of land? Use your imagination to create a clear picture of your new home. When you have done this, visualize yourself standing outside of your home and get a sense of how it feels to live there on a day-to-day basis. Then let the image go.

2. Have a clear vision of where your home is. Choose an area you would like to live in. If you do not have a specific area in mind, where would you prefer to be situated: in the country, close to the city, in the city, by the ocean, next to a lake, on the river, near woods, inside a forest? Are you located miles away from the nearest neighbor, or within a few feet? Do you approach your new home from a main road, lane, avenue, or dirt track? If there is a particular area you would like to live in, it is essential that you are clear about why you want to live there. For example, let's say you want to live in Manhattan because you will be close to work. What if a home in another area becomes available, just as close to work but not as desirable? If your dream home manifests in the wrong area, decide whether or not to take the home, or go through the manifestation process again, this time paying more attention to the location aspect of your wish.

3. The price is right! You make your wish—the home of your dreams is on the market, but the price is outside of your budget— what do you do? You can either manifest more money or be sure to include "within my price range" in your wish. The laws of manifestation are beyond the limitation of your beliefs. The only thing holding you back is your belief that you cannot have what you want. Until you let go of this limiting belief, your wish has to be believable to be achievable.

Once you have a clear picture of what you want, go through the wish sense process and use the Pink Bubble meditation in principle three to bring the essence of your wish into reality. Always include yourself in the visualization and remember to be realistic. You cannot manifest something that your mind cannot accept. Meanwhile, love the home you have and be grateful for all the blessings in your life. Although this complex wish takes time to manifest, your needs will always be met. If you need a new home immediately, just visualize what you need, let it go, and leave the rest to the universe.

When two people make a joint decision, it's often arrived at by compromise or surrender, although this was not the case with my friends Paul and Sally. They each had their own ideas about the perfect home. He wanted a townhouse, and she wanted a cottage. He imagined a courtyard, while Sally envisioned a rose and herb garden. Until they came to an agreement, no amount of wish sense was going to help the situation. So they independently wrote a list of what each most wanted in the ideal home. Paul wanted comfort, easy access to his work and friends, and the least amount of work on upkeep. Sally wanted a family home, warm and inviting, with lots of space outside and a garden. Neither of them could imagine what this perfect house could look like. So instead, they blended their ideas together and visualized being in a house that made each of them happy.

A few weeks later, a house came on the market that seemed to fit their wish. It was in a housing community that had maintenance programs for homeowners and was within a reasonable distance from Paul's work. The interior was warm and inviting with all the right touches to keep them both happy. It was situated next to a park and had a small and easily maintainable rose garden in front. But Sally also wanted an herb garden. The remarkable thing was that the morning they were due to look at the house, the current owner had received a gift—a box of herbs that she had placed on the patio. The couple took this to be a sign that they had found their new home.

Wishing for Good Health

Making a wish for material things such as more money, a new home, a vacation, or a promotion, can be achieved through wish sense with very little effort on your part. However, the next two wishes, for good health and a way of being, are more complicated because they involve deeper personal and emotional issues, such as how you feel about yourself. While the other wishes you make may also contain these issues, the intention behind this kind of wish is focused more within. Many wishes are focused externally, even if the essence of the wish is internal. So when you wish for a love relationship, your intention is to ask for a partner, yet your focus may also be on loving yourself. By focusing on yourself, you automatically open your heart to inviting a partner into your life.

You are not just a physical body; you are a complex being. It is important to know what you are striving for when you wish for good health. Health, as defined by the World Health Organization, is "a state of complete physical, mental, and social well-being and not merely absence of disease or infirmity." In other words, when you wish for good health, you are asking to be in an ideal state.

In order to achieve an ideal state, you need to remember that there are different levels of your being: physical, mental, emotional, and spiritual. If you wish for good health, be prepared to play your part in the process. You can imagine yourself healthy, healed, and whole, but if you are eating junk food, lazing around the house, thinking negative thoughts, and not living an authentic life, then your wish may only be realized in part, because you are not keeping your side of the bargain. If you constantly abuse your system, your wish might be short-lived. Remember the lottery joke about the guy who wanted to win the lottery and God said he had to buy the ticket in order to win? This is a similar situation. A wish for good health is a two-way street. Play your part in the process, and the universe will lend a helping hand by granting your wish.

Wishing for good health does work; the most important thing to do when you make your wish is to visualize yourself healthy, whole, and doing all the things you want to do with your life. Your unconscious mind has to be able to accept good health, although sometimes a health challenge is meant to be a part of one's life.

Those suffering long-term illnesses can sometimes hold the belief that they have attracted an illness to them. The laws of attraction obviously attract energy to us; that is the whole point. But this does not give people permission to blame themselves or someone else for an illness. There are many reasons for illness, and there are many masters or aspects governing that one law of attraction.

I fell ill a few years ago with typhoid fever and salmonella poisoning. At the time, I did not understand the reason for my state of health, but intuitively I received healing and inner guidance from a source that I call my spirit guide. My guide told me that illness is the sacred fire, and there are a multitude of reasons for it showing up in our lives. Fire is the creative element often associated with spirit, life, and the greater fire of creativity—the Divine or God. Illness—fiery energy—can relate to a vast amount of energy that has been withheld, like a rumbling volcano, and can be connected with an intense emotional event.

As I lay in bed with the typhoid fever, I began to understand some of the reasons we have illnesses. After my recovery, I made a list of those reasons and shared them as an article in a monthly newsletter I write for my website. This generated the largest response ever to any of my newsletters. We are so quick, especially in this New Age society, to think that we are to blame for illness. We are not. It may be a part of the package deal of this life, or it could be a "contract," as medical intuitive Caroline Myss likes to call it. Whatever it is, illness is there to show us something about ourselves that can be revealed through that suffering. It may also be the only way for us to bring some part of ourselves to the surface. Below is a partial list of the deeper motivations behind illness:

1. It gives us the attention and love we need.
2. We can learn something about ourselves. For example, colds can often signify blocked emotions, unreleased tears, and pain.
3. It can bring together people who have previously been separated for one reason or another.
4. We can help those around us to open their hearts to unconditional love through helping us.

5. We can learn how to cure it or/and help others to cure it.

6. We could meet certain people we were destined to meet and connect with.

7. It can help us to open different levels of our being that would have lain dormant or would have taken longer for us to open up to.

8. Illness shows us something we have neglected to look at or to heal within our psyche.

9. It can invite us to take stock of and completely change our lives.

10. Illness can help us to appreciate just how wonderful life is when we are healthy.

11. We often act like human doings instead of human beings, so illness does us a favor and helps us to slow down and reflect upon our lives.

Sometimes the reason we have an illness is just so we can experience getting better. Instead of judging the reasons why, look instead for the gift in the illness. Consider not only how you benefit, but how those around you profit, too. Don't blame the illness for being part of your life or yourself for attracting it. On some level you have chosen it, albeit unconsciously. Remember the bigger picture: there is often more to illness than meets the eye.

Your body has an innate intelligence and always strives toward healing and health. Healing does not necessarily mean to cure; it means to make whole. Making whole does not always mean getting better, but on some level it equals a release of energy that has been stored up and may have contributed to an illness. Some people are miraculously cured. People such as the Brazilian healer John of God have been a conduit for what we consider miracle cures. To be cured means that we have to be ready to let go of the illness, and to let go of the reasons for it. And sometimes there is even more asked of us than simply letting go into our illness. Sometimes we must let go into death.

So why not embrace your health in all of its states, accepting and learning from illness? In so doing you can take the necessary steps to let it go. Healing may require years, or maybe it will take a matter of seconds. Try not to judge your ability to heal against the passage of time. Time is but an illusion. Maybe on some other dimension of time, you are already completely cured, can live for thousands of years, or have parts that constantly regenerate. Maybe we live in the dimension of illness and some other part of our consciousness lives in a dimension of light where there is no illness. Maybe by keeping the illness you are healing other parts of yourself that need to be healed. Try to go with the flow of this, let go of any blame, and thank your body for supporting you on this journey. You can also tell your body that you are ready to let this illness go.

If you have an "incurable illness," visualize a doctor or a healer who knows exactly how to treat you and has the ability to affect a miracle cure. All things are possible within the realm of your imagination. Good health wishes can be difficult because they are personal, and it can be more difficult to let go of a personal wish. Despite this, visualize it in the here and now; then let go, and trust in the process.

Wishing for a New Way of Being

I have always admired nice people, those who see the positive and who are incapable of uttering a nasty word about anyone or anything. I consider this to be quite an achievement. Unfortunately, being nice does not just happen to you. It is a way of being. Any wish for something that is designed to alter the way you are, the way you think, or the way you act can be accomplished, and achieving it is often an ongoing process.

Begin by changing any beliefs that do not serve you or your vision of yourself. Beliefs such as "I am not good enough" or "I am unattractive" or "I am unworthy" can stop you from accomplishing the new way of being you desire. Some of the ways to transform these beliefs and habits have already been explored earlier in the book. However, there are a few other techniques you can incorporate into your habit-breaking regimen.

The first is taken from Donna Eden's book, *Energy Medicine*, and employs something called the temporal tap. This is an ancient technique to relieve pain that has also been found to be an effective method for breaking patterns. Decide on a belief or habit you would like to change. Create a statement to bring about this change, and construct it in a way that includes a negative word such as *don't, never, can't, won't, no,* and so forth. While you repeat your statement, tap around your left ear using the three middle fingers of your left hand, traveling from the temporal bone, around the back of the ear, and finishing at the base of your earlobe. Repeat your statement once for each round of taps, repeating the round six times. When you have finished the left ear, do the same thing to your right ear, but this time use a positive statement.

For example, if you think you are unattractive, tap around your left ear, "I no longer consider myself to be unattractive," and around the right ear, "I am extremely attractive and beautiful." It is essential to make your statement in the present tense. Experiment with this. If it does not work, try changing your statement and then try it again, but give it time to sink in. Do the temporal tap twice a day for at least a week and see if you notice any change. Some people will have instantaneous results, while others will take longer.

Visualize how you would like this new way of being to be for you. If you want to be more peaceful, visualize yourself in a garden, at peace with the world. If you would like to be wiser, imagine that you are a teacher with students amazed at the insights you give them, and envision their happy faces as they leave after your counsel. If you want to be more loving, visualize a line of people waiting to receive love and hugs from you; really get a sense of the elation this brings for both yourself and others. If you want to bring forgiveness into your life, you can either visualize yourself as a forgiving person or you can picture yourself talking to the person you need to forgive.

Cutting Cord Connections

The Cutting Cord Connections technique is an adapted exercise from Phyllis Krystal's wonderful book *Cutting the Ties That Bind*. In it, she describes an exercise to help to release energy associated with our relationship to others. The premise is that in each relationship we create energy cords that are similar to umbilical cords. Each cord signifies the consciousness within the relationship—how it was created, how the energy flows between the people involved, and how each is reacting to that energy. I see these cords as light filaments resembling a laser show. Often, when there are many people, the cords build a network in the center of the group, reminiscent of a spider's web. These cords have been created since birth, some before birth. They can hold us in patterns and beliefs that no longer serve us, as well as attaching us to relationships that we have outgrown.

WISH PRACTICE:
Cutting Cord Connections

☆ ★ ★ ☆ ★ ☆ ★ ☆ ★ ★ ☆ ★ ☆ ★ ☆ ★ ★ ☆ ★ ☆ ★ ☆

This exercise is an active meditation, meaning that you are actively processing energy as you create images in your mind. It uses the image of a figure eight. This image is symbolic of many things, but most significantly it is the sign most often associated with infinity and is numerologically representative of the planet Saturn, the lord of time. Personally, I associate Saturn with karmic energy, so we can see that the figure eight has a great many parallel energies associated with it. Phyllis Krystal considers it a protective image, one that creates an individual's space while avoiding invasion of another's space.

Begin by finding a comfortable position. Close your eyes and take a few deep breaths, allowing yourself to be in this present moment, grounded and centered. Now think of the person you wish to change the energy with. It might be a family member, an old love, or your boss. Visualize a figure eight of white light, with violet light in the center of each zero. Violet is the color of transformation, and white is the color of cleansing. Put the person you want to release or need to forgive in one side of the figure eight and put yourself in the other half. Make yourself comfortable, and have a conversation. Talk about the good and bad points of your relationship, say whatever needs to be said, and then thank this person for agreeing to be in relationship with you.

Once you have done this, and if it feels appropriate, use your intuition to visualize the cords that each of you have created in the relationship. Imagine that you have in your hands a pair of golden scissors, and one by one cut the energy cords, allowing each part of the cord to heal up and return to its respective owner. When you have finished cutting the cords, turn your attention to the figure eight. Using your golden scissors, cut the figure eight in half, allowing each half to become a whole circle, and then see the person you have released or forgiven drift away into the distance as you let go.

Do this exercise as many times as you need to. You can also visualize and change the events that led up to your need to release energy or forgive. Use the Stepping Out meditation in chapter 4 to help you to do this. Alternatively, design your own meditation. Just be open to the signs, do not judge yourself, and allow yourself the luxury of a new way of being.

✩ ★ ✭ · ☆ · ✩ ★ ✭ · ☆ · ✩ ★ ✭ · ☆ · ✩

Jon was a client who had worked most of his life in an office. He was an ordinary guy, living in a townhouse, working the required forty hours a week, and a little overweight. He didn't have any goals and didn't see the point in making any changes. He came to one of my introductory workshops at the request of a work colleague, a bright soul who was interested in helping others.

Jon listened to my pitch, took part in the exercises, and appeared untouched by the energy of the evening. The following year I offered another introductory workshop in the same location. Jon was there again. I only recognized him because I remembered his curly and out-of-control hair. It transpired that after the previous workshop, he had gone home and started to think about what he most wanted in his life. He hadn't thought about it before because no one had asked him to think about it. He had made a list of all the things he wanted, and then a list of all the things he hadn't previously allowed himself to want.

Having made his lists, Jon, who was typically a solitary person, noticed that he felt drawn to a female coworker. However, one of his wishes was to experience peace, and something intuitively told him that this woman had the key to the manifestation of his wish. It turned out that she had an interest in complementary medicine and provided Jon with the self-help books and meditation CDs that literally catapulted him into another state of awareness. He noticed that the more he read, and understood who he was, the more people began to talk to him. He found himself discussing topics that he previously had no interest in, yet now they were defining him.

This newly found peace initiated a desire to care for his body. He took up yoga, became conscious of the food he ate, and began to lose weight. During the next year his whole being, attitude, health, and way of life changed. He remembered that before his greater sense of peace, he had held a longing in his heart for something new, something different in his life, but he had not allowed himself to cherish this wish. It was the spark of desire alone that had manifested a series of events leading to the wonderful changes he was experiencing. He had expected to find peace in a different way. Instead, he discovered that his life reflected his inner world and that what he had been searching for was already there within him, waiting to be found.

9

Wish Quest

Celebrate what you want to see more of.
—Thomas J. Peters

Now look back at your original wish—the one you made on your wish card. Is this really what you want, or are you yearning for something else? It may help at this point to read through your wish journal. Your insights, highlighted words, and experiences will help you to focus your attention on the nature of your wish. If you want to change the wish or reconstruct it in some way, the information contained within your wish journal will help you to design the right wish for you. If you are happy with your original wish, then follow the steps to make it happen. When you have done this, put the card back inside the envelope, seal it, and place it somewhere special in your home. Act as if you have already been assured of your wish. Then forget about it.

Luck, Coincidence, or Pure Magic?

Luck has no part in the manifestation process. Throughout writing this book, I have been constantly reminded of the many occasions my wishes have been granted, even when the odds were stacked against their materialization. One such wish particularly sticks in my mind. I had been away from England for six months while traveling in Europe and had the daunting task of returning to my native land without a job or a home. A few days before I was due to arrive back in London, I telephoned a friend for some work advice. We had met while working at the same hospital, a job I left to pursue my travels. She had continued to work there, so I thought she might know of

165

any available jobs. I described the kind of job I wanted to her and explained that it would involve me making my own work schedule, caring for the same person every day, earning enough money to take the courses that I was interested in, and enabling me to travel whenever I wanted. She informed me that should a job like this exist, it would be unavailable to permanent members of staff—it allowed too much flexibility and would only be offered to temporary workers. I was considered permanent staff. All the same, I went through the process of wish sense and imagined myself in this position.

A few days later I arrived in England. I was fortunate enough to be able to stay with friends until I found a place of my own. Tired and weary, I deposited my luggage on the floor of their apartment, ready to put my feet up for a well-deserved rest. The sofa looked inviting. I turned to make my way toward the comforting pillows when the telephone was thrust into my hand by my host with orders to call my colleague at the hospital as soon as possible. My colleague had left a cryptic message: "Your wish has been granted."

At first I had no idea what she meant, but then I remembered telling her of my job wish and excitedly dialed her number. There was indeed a job available exactly as I had described and, for the first time, permanent members of staff were eligible to apply for the position. She could not believe my luck. I was offered the job and was able to have the freedom that I needed—everything I had wished for was available to me.

Luck is really another word for coincidence, and we know that there are no coincidences, don't we? It has been said that coincidences are anomalies in time, designed to reveal that you are traveling in the right direction. In other words, going with the flow of energy rather than against it creates pockets of energy related to our deepest wishes, and this certainly worked for me.

Often, when you are most in need of advice or guidance, someone appears as if by magic and helps you. This is not a coincidence, nor is it luck. We attract everything to us, so by making a wish you are focusing your energy toward something and saying, "This is what I most want in my life." Being open to receive is the next step. So when you need advice and make a silent wish for help, be sure to remain open to receiving the help you so desire. Dr. Wayne Dyer says, "Align your purpose with the field of intention," which is a rather technical way of saying that your energy moves toward what you focus on, and what you focus on can indeed manifest, just as all your wishes and dreams can come true.

A Wish Comes True

Put as many wishes on your wish list as you desire, and cross off each wish as it comes true. From time to time, you will need to make a new list as your priorities and tastes change. Keep a diary of your wishes, no matter how small. Record when you made the wish and how long it took to manifest. As you use your innate ability to influence energy, you will notice that your wishes materialize with greater speed and regularity. You are the center of your universe; you have the creative power to control everything that goes on around you in your world. Everyone has the ability to manifest his or her desires. It takes belief in yourself, not in something outside of yourself, to prime your powers of manifestation.

As you become more accustomed to using your wish sense powers, you will begin to notice that some wishes manifest almost instantaneously in spite of their apparent complexity. One year I spent a week alone on Jekyll Island in South Carolina while my husband was in Florida working for Habitat for Humanity. Most of my time was spent cycling around the island and walking on the beach. There was very little to do there. One day as I passed the airport, I thought how nice it would be to fly in one of the small airplanes. I imagined the experience and then let the image go. A short while later, I passed a man on roller blades who looked lost. I stopped to ask if he needed any help. He told me that he was looking for a particular hotel. I directed him to the hotel, but instead of parting ways we chatted for a while. It transpired that he had arrived in his own light aircraft and only had roller blades for transportation. He invited me to lunch and, after we spent a few hours together, he invited me to take a trip in his airplane! Now that you have the formula for making all of your wishes come true, this kind of thing can happen to you, too.

About Being Perfect

There are no failures, just feedback. Each experience helps us to discover the best way for us to be in relationship with our deeper desires. Thomas Edison reportedly made over six thousand faulty lightbulbs until he discovered the right way to make a lightbulb. When on one occasion he was challenged by a young journalist who inquired as to why he had made so many mistakes, he replied, "Young man, don't you realize that I have not failed but have successfully discovered six thousand ways that won't work!"

You will learn through your own experience how to make a wish. If you think that you are incapable of making your wishes come true, or that there are too many obstacles in your life to allow your wish to manifest, then think again. We all have our challenges to overcome in life, but with persistence we can achieve anything we desire. Queen Elizabeth's father, King George, had a speech impediment, yet this did not stop him from speaking in public. His was a position that obligated him to come under constant scrutiny from the public eye. You can do anything you put your mind to—include your heart and you hold within you the recipe for success.

Unmanifested Wishes

If your wish does not manifest, look back at your reasons for making it in the first place. Check that you are asking for the right thing, and then go through the process again. Some wishes take longer than others. There is no telling whether your wish will be here next week, next year, or a few years down the line. Have faith that you will receive what you need at any given moment in your life. You have put your energy out there, and like a boomerang it will return, in one form or another. Do remember to be careful what you ask for because you might just get it.

The Master Wish Maker

When you become a master wish maker, you can apply another technique called the Stepping-Stone Surprise to determine what you need to wish for. When I decided to leave the nursing profession, I made up my mind that I wanted to work as a healer. I began working and traveling with one of the world's most amazing healers, and yet I could not manifest the next step. I decided to meditate on what this next step included.

This stepping-stone technique came to me in my hour of need, and I tested it for its usefulness. I visualized stepping-stones from my situation in that moment to my objective as a healer. The first stone appeared to be too far away to jump to, so I imagined a tight-rope between my stone and the next. After that I visualized the potential tightrope length of each of the modalities that I could incorporate into my work. To my surprise, I saw that healing could only produce half of a tightrope, and yet when I integrated intuitive counseling with healing, the tightrope stretched from my stone to the next. With this information now available to me, I made it my intention to work as an intuitive counselor and healer; as soon as I did this, everything fell into place.

Although you will discover your own way of manifesting wishes, you will almost certainly incorporate the key formula of the Seven Principles into your wish sense technique. Eventually this system will become second nature to you, and you will have earned the title of master wish maker.

Use the Stepping-Stone Surprise technique to determine how to get from the place you are now to the place you want to be. Used in the right way, this information will help you to manifest whatever you want in your life. This is not just about finding the way from where you are now to where you want to go, but a willingness to see the next step of your journey. It is a choice, and once you make that choice the next step will appear.

WISH PRACTICE:
Stepping-Stone Surprise

☆ ★ ★ ☆ ・ ☆ ・ ☆ ★ ★ ☆ ・ ☆ ・ ☆ ★ ★ ☆ ・ ☆ ・ ☆

First, formulate a question in your mind. This technique works best when you want to get from A to Z. It shows you the steps to take to get to Z, such as step B or step C. On a piece of paper make a circle on one side with the heading Where I Am Now in big letters. Place in here where you are in this moment. If the question is about a job, then write the title of your job. If it is about a relationship, then write down the name of the other person or the kind of situation you are in. On the other side of the paper, draw another circle with the heading My Destination and write in here what your destination is— a new job, new relationship, etc. You can use the technique I described earlier to help you to get from the first stepping-stone to your destination. Remember to close your eyes and center yourself first. Use your imagination to help you get from this one stone to your destination.

If visualizing the stones in this way docs not work, then try this instead: Close your eyes, center yourself, and ask, "Between one and ten, how many steps will it take for me to go from where I am now to arrive at my destination?" Be open to whatever number comes up for you. If your mind chooses a number greater than ten, then go with that. Once you have this number, either count up to this number in a written list, or draw that number of stepping-stones from where you are now to where you are heading. Then close your eyes and center yourself again. This time ask yourself, "What is the first stepping-stone?" Imagine jumping from the stone you are standing on to the next one. What does it take for you to get from one stone to another? Once you have the answer, you can either open your eyes to write it down on the first stepping-stone, or you can continue on with the exercise until you arrive at your destination. If you decide to go with the later technique, make the intention to retain all the information you receive during the exercise.

✫ ⋆ ★ ⋆ ✫ ⋆ ☆ ⋆ ✫ ⋆ ★ ⋆ ✫ ⋆ ☆ ⋆ ✫ ⋆ ★ ⋆ ✫ ⋆ ☆ ⋆ ✫

Fulfilling Your Heart's Desires

Open your heart to receive everything you have ever dreamed of—because you deserve it. You are the magician, the creator who can mold energies into form. There was nothing in existence until you created it. Remember who you are, where you came from, and where you are going. And on the way, realize your dreams, actualize your desires, and manifest your wishes.

My Wish for You ...

That your wishes manifest.
That you have what you need in this life to make you happy.
That you receive and accept everything you deserve.

Happy Wishing!

Wish you were here ...

Let us know of your experiences with wish sense and any successful techniques you may have developed using the methods in this book. When you receive the manifestation of your original wish, or the revised version of it, let me know. Include information on how long it took for your wish to manifest and the techniques of wish sense that worked best for you. For a full list of meditation CDs, workshop schedules, forthcoming books, and contact information, visit my website at www.sealedwithlove.com.

Recommended Reading

Author unknown, foreword by Cyril Scott. *The Boy Who Saw True*. London: Rider, 2005.

Burgess, Alan. *The Small Woman: The True Story of Gladys Aylward of China*. Ann Arbor, MI: Servant Publications, 1984.

Coelho, Paulo. *The Alchemist*. New York: HarperCollins, 2006.

Eden, Donna. *Energy Medicine*. London: Piatkus Books, 2003.

Emoto, Dr. Masaru. *The Hidden Messages of Water*. Hillsboro, OR: Beyond Words, 2004.

Hay, Louise L. *You Can Heal Your Life*. Carlsbad, CA: Hay House, 1984.

Jampolsky, M.D., Gerald G. *Love Is Letting Go of Fear*. Berkeley, CA: Celestial Arts, 2004.

Jeffers, Susan. *Feel the Fear . . . and Do It Anyway*. New York: Ballantine Books, 2006.

Krystal, Phyllis. *Cutting the Ties That Bind*. Bangalore, India: Sri Sathya Sai Hotels Pvt Ltd, 1999.

MacDonald-Bayne, Murdo. *The Higher Power You Can Use*. Christchurch, New Zealand: Mystica Publications, 2006.

Spezzano, Chuck. *50 Ways to Change Your Mind and Change the World*. London: Hodder & Stoughton, 2002.

Talbot, Michael. *The Holographic Universe*. New York: HarperCollins, 1996.

Williamson, Marianne. *A Return to Love: Reflections on the Principles of a Course in Miracles*. New York: HarperCollins, 1996.